DRY
FLIES

DRY FLIES

An Improved Method of Tying

L. T. THREADGOLD

SWAN·HILL PRESS

First published in the UK in 1998
by Swan Hill Press, an imprint of Airlife Publishing Ltd

British Library Cataloguing-in-Publication Data
  A catalogue record for this book
  is available from the British Library

ISBN 1 85310 993 2

Typeset by Phoenix Typesetting, Ilkley, West Yorkshire
Printed in Hong Kong

Swan Hill Press
an imprint of Airlife Publishing Ltd
101 Longden Road, Shrewsbury, SY3 9EB, England

Dedication

To Vincent Marinaro whose inspired writings have given me innumerable vivid insights into the worlds of the trout, the fly and the fisherman.

Acknowledgements

I am happy to confess that the parentage and inspiration for this text lie with the seminal books *The Trout and the Fly* by Brian Clarke and John Goddard and *To Rise a Trout* by John Roberts. The influence which the ideas and information contained in these two books had on my attitude and approach to dry-fly fishing for trout was nothing less than revolutionary. I am ever grateful that these authors put pen to paper. John Goddard's book *Trout Fly Recognition* has also been a source of inspiration and a text to which I return repeatedly. Furthermore, John Goddard helped me resolve a number of problems I had about fish vision by most generously allowing me to see a preliminary typescript of the vision section of his forthcoming book; this greatly assisted me in writing my own chapters on this topic.

I have tried to push forward the frontiers established by the authors listed above in three ways: first by giving greater anatomical detail concerning the piscean eye (without, I hope, making such information indigestible to the layman), second, by extending the illustration of the views which the trout has of both the underwater and above water worlds from two to three dimensions and third by the development of a method of tying dry flies which was inspired by the experiments and critical evaluation of fly-tying systems by the aforementioned authors, coupled with the inspired writings of Vincent Marinaro.

Finally, it is with the greatest pleasure that I acknowledge my debt to Professor Bill Muntz, Monash University, Australia for his expert advice and help with the topic of fish vision and related matters, for his input largely determined the contents of the first two chapters. Professor Muntz has been most free and generous with his time and on numerous occasions has pointed me in the right direction with respect to the relevant literature, as well as ensuring I did not make some elementary errors; any errors remaining I lay claim to in full!

L.T. Threadgold

Introduction

Like many a fly-fisherman who ties his own flies I have been greatly influenced by three texts. Firstly, Clarke and Goddard's book, *The Trout and the Fly*, particularly the sections dealing with trout vision and the new fly tyings they describe. Secondly by John Roberts' *To Rise a Trout*, especially for his critical appraisal and evaluation of a very broad range of fly patterns and tying methods. Finally, and I acknowledge most profoundly, by Vincent Marinaro's *In the Ring of the Rise*, a book demonstrating acute observational powers, great originality of thought and an outstandingly inventive mind. On the basis of these accounts I have for some years been tying experimental fly patterns which have modifications of both hackles and wings. Many patterns proved complete failures on the water even though they looked promising on the bench and others were only uncertain catchers of fish, initially promising but in the long term no better than other, more conventional, patterns. Only with the development of the 'Footprint Fly' described in this book have I managed to produce flies which are easy to tie and which are attractive to trout under a wide range of conditions.

Since I now believe the patterns I fish are giving the required stimulatory signals in the correct sequence, I have greater confidence in them and consequently my fishing has become more enjoyable. I sincerely hope the reader of this text will in due course reap similar rewards. Nevertheless two points must be made about the patterns described in this book. The first point is that these patterns are not in any sense the 'ultimate' dry flies, for the book's title, *An Improved Tying Method* has been carefully chosen. I do not doubt that improvements by other fly tiers on my improved method will be made and very possibly a totally new system using as yet untried materials will eventually appear. Similarly the use of these patterns will not prove a panacea. Waving a Footprint Fly at the end of your fishing wand will not magically turn a tyro into an expert or a moderately successful fisherman into a master. However, their use should induce more rises and so afford more opportunities to savour the thrill of a taut line. Unfortunately watercraft and casting skill, observation and thought, knowledge and understanding, persistence and experience are still the major influences for fishing success. Even the most exact imitation of the natural fly will not alter that situation one jot!

Contents

Chapter 1

In the Eye of the Beholder – Trout Vision

The fly tier's objective ever since the invention of the dry fly has been to produce an artificial with the characteristics of the natural fly which stimulate trout to rise and take. But what are the essential features of natural floating flies which trout find irresistible? Until relatively recently this question could not be answered comprehensively because our knowledge of fish vision and the anatomical and physiological aspects of the piscean eye were not sufficiently detailed. Trial and error, experience over many years, tradition and word-of-mouth, the success or failure of a pattern in the hands of experts and amateurs alike, allied to an understanding of entomology, were the only criteria for the modification of existing patterns or the origin of new ones.

In order to appreciate the new tyings described in subsequent chapters, the reader will find it an advantage to understand the extent to which the patterns were determined by the characteristics, qualities and limitations of fish vision; in other words how the trout sees in general, especially in relation to the air-water interface and how it sees the fly as it floats towards it on the surface film.

The Structure of the Piscean Eye

The trout's eyes are placed latero-frontally on the head above the posterior half of the upper scissors of the jaw, in line with the nostrils. They are tilted slightly inwards towards the front and upwards (fig. 1). The eyes are circular in shape and only slightly convex, so lying virtually flush with the streamlined surface of the head. There are no eyelids and consequently the eyes are permanently 'open'. The eyeballs lie in ellipsoidal sockets which allow some forward and backward tilting of the eyes but little up-and-down movement. The eye has external muscles so that the yaw, pitch and roll of the fish results in compensatory movements of the eye which tend to stabilise the image on the retina. The existence of these slight movements is usually ignored

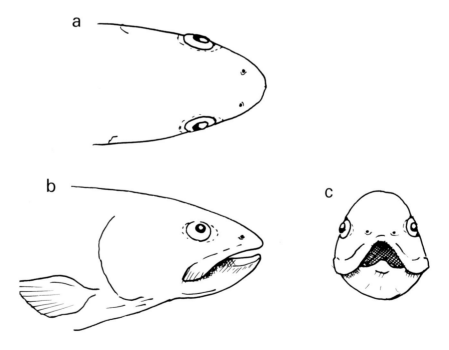

Figure 1   The position of the eyes of a trout as viewed from (a) above, (b) laterally and (c) in front.

14

in fishing texts but they may have a bearing on both monocular and binocular vision by allowing a greater range of focusing than might be supposed.

Anatomy

The piscean eye is similar to that of the human in its essential components but differs in certain specifics. The eye has a clear cornea which is slightly convex and continuous with the cartilaginous sclera which forms the hemispherical back of the eye

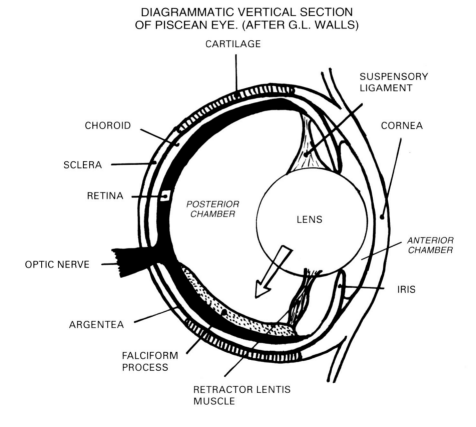

DIAGRAMMATIC VERTICAL SECTION
OF PISCEAN EYE. (AFTER G.L. WALLS)

Figure 2   Vertical section of the eye of a fish. Note particularly the retractor lentis muscle and the large arrow pointing to the general direction in which the lens moves when the muscle contracts.

15

(fig. 2). The cornea is covered externally by a clear layer of skin which includes the conjunctiva. The cornea in fish does not act as the first focusing unit of the eye as it does in man, for whom the lens is a secondary fine focusing device.

The spherical lens is held between an elastic ligament above and the retractor lentis muscle below (fig. 2). It is composed of living cells and encapsulated by a very thin layer of other cells, so that it grows along with the fish itself. The lens has a very small focal length of approximately 2.5 times its radius.

The front face of the lens projects through the circular iris, the golden ring round the dark centre of the eye, and lies close to the cornea. Consequently the anterior chamber of the eye is very small (fig. 2). The lens is not homogeneous for the highest re-fractive index is at its centre and the refractive index falls off progressively to the periphery (fig. 3A). If this were not the case then the lens would show spherical aberration (light rays passing through different parts of the lens would not all focus at the same point) (fig. 3B). The lens is uncorrected for chromatic aberration (different colours of light focusing at different points on the retina due to their different wavelengths) but it is assumed that the fish brain can cope with this distortion as do humans. Furthermore, at any depth of water there is a reduction in the spectral (colour) range of the light reaching the fish's eye so that the problem becomes less important. This fact would to some extent reduce the importance of the colour of natural and artifi-cial flies.

The fish's eye is focused not by altering the lens shape as in man but by moving the lens closer to the retina by means of the retractor lentis muscle (fig. 2). However, this simple statement must be amplified because:

- The retina is not spherical but slightly ellipsoidal since its antero-posterior axis (major axis) is some 3% longer than the vertical one (minor axis).
- The contraction of the retractor lentis muscle moves the lens not towards the centre of the retina (fundus), but backwards in a line almost parallel to the antero-posterior axis of the fish's body (fig. 2).

In a fair-sized trout the semi-elliptical retina is 10.3 mm along the major axis and 10 mm along the minor one. The centre of the

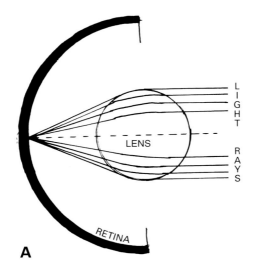

A

Figure 3
A. The different refractive indices in different parts of the spherical lens of a trout.

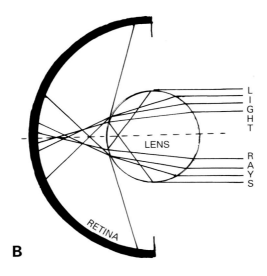

B

B. The lack of focus (spherical aberration) which would result if the refractive index of all parts of the lens of a trout were the same.

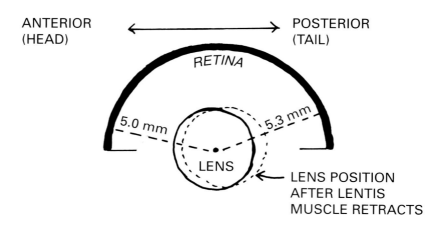

Figure 4   *A horizontal section of a trout's eye which illustrates the 'off-centre' position of the lens in relation to the anterior-posterior axis of the fish and the movement of the lens when the lentis muscle retracts.*

spherical lens at rest is 5 mm from the fundus and anterior margins of the retina but 5.3 mm from the posterior part of the retina (fig. 4). (Example taken from R.J. Pumphrey. See Bibliography.) When the retractor lentis muscle contracts, it pulls the lens nearer to the temporal quadrant of the retina and so brings remote objects ahead and above into focus (figs 2 and 4). The distance of the lens to the remainder of the retina is virtually unchanged, so no focusing is possible for other directions of view.

A circular iris defines the back of the anterior chamber and is in contact with the front face of the lens. The iris has a fixed aperture and cannot be opened and closed in response to changes in light intensity as occurs in man. It is for this reason that trout seek deeper water or shade when sunlight is intense, even though there are alterations in the light receptive retinal cells themselves and the dark pigment of the adjacent pigment cells migrates up between them; both these are protective devices against strong light. The iris is continuous with a silvery layer (the argentea), which lines the inside of the sclera. Between the silvery layer and the innermost light-sensitive layer, the retina, is the choroid, a complex of blood vessels which supplies the retina. Near the entrance of the optic nerve at the back of the eye, a vascular fold of the choroid (the falciform process) penetrates the retina, crosses the posterior chamber and ends as a knob attached to the back of the lens; it presumably supplies oxygen and nutrients to the living, growing lens (fig. 2).

The retina forms the innermost layer of the eye which lines the posterior chamber and contains two types of light-receptor cells: the rods, which operate well in dim light and can detect contrast and movement, but not colour or detail, and the cones which are effective in bright light and detect colour and detail. In fish the cones are more widely distributed over the entire retina than in man (in whom they are concentrated in a small area), so forming a mosaic. The reason for this is that, unlike man, fish cannot readily move the head from side to side. Furthermore the trout's eye has relatively more rods and fewer cones than the eye of man so that it works better in dim light, is very responsive to movement and contrast but is not as capable of discerning fine detail or subtle differences in shades of colour. The trout's eye is therefore well adapted to an environment in which light penetrates less well than in air.

The neural parts of the light-receptor cells and the intermediate nerve cells and plexuses which line the inner face of the retina next to the posterior chamber connect the rods and cones to the optic nerve which exits from the back of the eye just below its centre. The vertebrate eye is inverted, with the nerves conducting impulses from the eye to the brain being nearer to the lens than the photo-receptors (rods and cones), which are the nerve cells which actually perceive and respond to light rays. During embryological development the eye develops first as a ball on a stalk extension of the forebrain, but at a later stage of development the front face of the ball 'folds' inwards until it is in contact with the back wall, hence the eye becomes inverted.

There are two basic classes of visual pigment in the cells of the retina, one absorbing light of short wavelengths and the other light at longer wavelengths. The first class of pigment predominates in the upper part of the retina and so this part is adapted for looking downwards where blues and greens predominate, whereas the second class of pigment predominates in the inferior (lower) half of the eye and so is adapted for looking upwards and responding to the longer wavelengths of red, orange and yellow.

Chapter 2

Visions Near and Far

The Trout's Perception of the Environment

The trout's vision of the underwater and above-water worlds is determined by two factors, first refraction, that is the bending of light rays as they pass from a medium of one density to a medium of a different density and second, the positioning of its own eyes in relation to its body.

Light rays passing through the air and penetrating into the water show no bending if viewed as coming from immediately overhead by the underwater observer, i.e. if the rays are vertically downwards. However, as the rays enter from larger angles from the vertical towards the horizontal, the bending increases until 10° is reached (fig. 5). Below 10° such a small amount of light enters the water and images are so distorted that this angle may be considered as a limiting one for the trout's view of the world above the water surface. The only images which are useful to a trout, therefore, are those that are more than 10° above the horizontal.

21

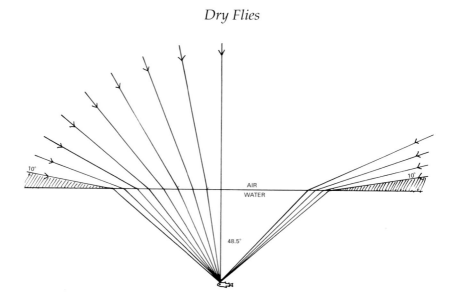

Figure 5   The trout's 160° arc of vision above the water surface is funnelled down to 97° below the water surface due to refraction. Below 10° from the horizontal is virtually a blind spot for the trout due to severe distortion of the image.

As a result of refraction the trout has an inverted cone of vision which has an angle of 97° at its tip which is located at the eyes. The base of the cone impinges on the water surface as a circular area called the 'window' (figs 6, 7 and 9). Although above the water surface the cone angle widens to an arc of 160° (i.e. the horizontal 180° less 10° for each side), to the trout the ground level is along the 48.5° line, that is apparently 'uphill' and well above the trout's head (fig 6).

Any ray of light with an angle in excess of 48.5° from the vertical is reflected back into the water and therefore the water surface acts essentially as a mirror (fig. 7). Consequently, outside the window the trout sees not the world above the water but a reflected image of the substratum and the associated physical surroundings. These reflected surroundings are called the mirror but the term is something of a misnomer since it suggests a uniformly silvered surface. In contrast the environment of a trout is not uniform and being composed of water, weeds, stones and

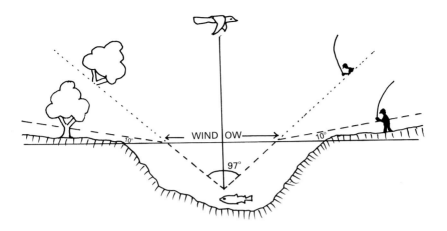

Figure 6 The trout's view of structures on the bank and in the air. The bird above the centre of the window appears true to size and shape. The fisherman and trees on the bank appear uphill along a projection of the underwater 48.5° limits of the trout's cone of vision.

substrata in varying shades ranging from white through blue and green to dark brown, the mirror is in consequence more often green, bluey-green, greeny-brown or brown. Only if the substrate is whitish, green vegetation sparse and the sky blue or grey will the mirror appear greyish. The silver-grey mirror seen in an aquarium full of static water is not the usual colour of the mirror in nature. Finally, it must be pointed out that although the mirror is in reality an unstable ceiling limited by whatever boundaries surround the water (fig. 7A), this is not how the trout sees it (fig. 7B). To the trout the mirror is a curved screen sloping to a 'horizon' in the middle distance (fig. 7B). To quote Clarke and Goddard's *The Trout and the Fly*, 'To the trout lying close to it, the mirror appears to slope sharply down around him like the roof of a bell tent with its top sliced off'. The trout's experience of this particular part of his environment is similar to our own, therefore, for to us our ceiling (the sky) seems to be a bowl, the rim of which touches the ground at the horizon; this appearance is of course an optical illusion just like the trout's sloping mirror.

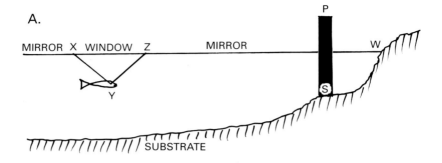

Figure 7
A. *A cross-sectional view of the edge of a lake. The trout lying at Y has a window X–Z with a mirror 'ceiling' to its left and right to W, which is a sort of 'horizon'. P–S is a wooden stake driven into the river's substratum, towards which the trout faces.*

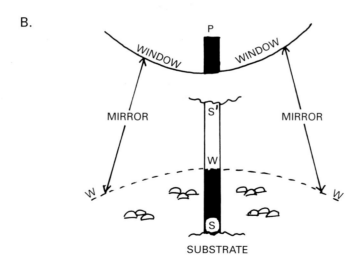

B. *The trout's view of the post, the top of which it sees in the window and the remainder at W–S. W–S¹ is the reflection of the lower part of the post in the mirror, which appears to the trout as a curved screen in which even the substrate will be reflected.*

Unfortunately, there is controversy concerning the 'bell tent'-like mirror. The accepted wisdom has been that if a fisherman is wading, the trout will see two pairs of legs – the real legs from substrate to mirror surface and the reflection of those legs in the mirror itself. In Ward's book, *Animals under Water* a photograph of a wading heron seen from underwater clearly shows four legs and feet, two real and two reflections. However, Clarke and Goddard state that no legs were visible in numerous photographs of fishermen wading to within 7 ft of a camera on the bed of the river and that this is due to the mirror sloping sharply down to an horizon in the near-middle distance.

It is difficult to reconcile these contradictory findings but a possible explanation is as follows: if a structure lies with its base inside the walls of the 'bell tent' (above the 'horizon'), then its length from the substrate to water surface should be visible to the trout along with its reflection in the mirror, i.e. every structure will appear twice as in fig. 8A. However, if the base of the structure lies outside the point where the 'bell tent' wall (the sloping mirror) appears to contact the horizon, then that structure will be 'invisible' to the trout for it will be over its 'horizon' (fig. 8A). The slope of the wall of the 'bell tent' is critical, therefore, but unfortunately this is unknown for any depth at which a fish might lie. Clarke and Goddard do not state whether their 'several dozen' photographs were a series taken starting very near the camera

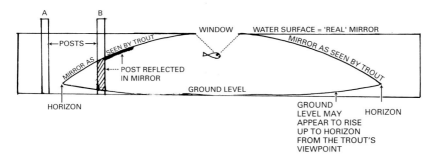

Figure 8A.   A cross-section of a piece of water showing the surroundings of the trout limited by the window, the 'curved' mirror and the apparent 'horizon' where mirror and ground level meet. Post A is beyond the 'horizon' and so invisible to the trout, whereas post B is within its 'horizon' and is therefore visible along with its mirror image.

25

and then at increasingly greater distances from it. Their text implies that no photograph was taken nearer than seven feet and consequently it may be that all their underwater photographs were of fishermen wading outside the 'bell tent' around the camera. Another possible solution is that if the camera used by Clarke and Goddard did not have a fish-eye lens and pointed directly upwards, then its view might not be the same as that of a fish and its 'horizon' might be very close to the camera. A resolution of this intriguing problem would be of considerable interest to fishermen.

The boundary between window and mirror is not a sharp one because some light enters at and below 10° as mentioned above. Instead, the boundary is an iridescent circle, called Snell's circle, which shows the spectrum from red nearest the mirror through orange, yellow, green, blue and violet; the orange and yellow bands are generally the most obvious (fig. 8B). The clarity of Snell's circle is controlled by the smoothness or otherwise of the

Figure 8B   Snell's circle. The mirror is at the bottom and the window at the top, with Snell's circle between. The red and orange bands of the spectrum are most evident but the green, blue and violet can be seen in the small insert. The blue/grey ill-defined figures at the extreme left and right-hand upper corners are bare trees some considerable distance away.

water surface, i.e. it is most sharp in a flat calm and most ill-defined when the surface is turbulent.

Because the trout's inverted cone of vision is fixed at 97°, the deeper it lies in the water the larger the diameter of its window at the surface (fig. 9). There is a disadvantage to this enlarged window, however, since at greater depth less light will reach the fish's eye. Objects immediately overhead of the trout are seen undistorted and true to size, but distortion increases and objects become wider and shorter as the boundary of the window is approached (fig. 6). Bankside features will appear more 'true' as the trout descends deeper in the water because such objects will appear nearer the centre of the window. The fisherman too is misled by refraction for trout appear further away from him than they really are and higher in the water; happily these facts are of no significance if the fisherman is casting to rising trout.

The second factor important in the trout's view of its environment both above and below water is the position of its own eyes and their physical characteristics. As already stated, the eyes are placed latero-frontally and inclined slightly inwards and upwards and the lens is spherical. This gives the fish a field of

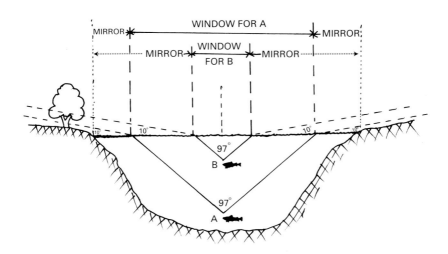

Figure 9   This sectional diagram shows the window and the mirror, and how the size of the former varies with the depth at which the trout lies in the water column.

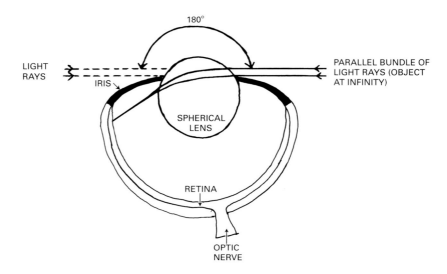

Figure 10   The spherical lens of a trout's eye allows it to have a sector of vision of some 180°.

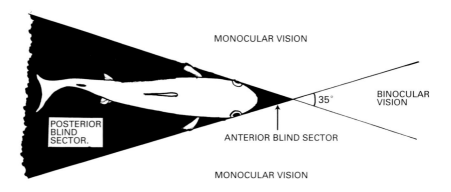

Figure 11   The sectors of monocular and binocular vision of a trout as viewed from directly above. The binocular sector has an angle of 35° and focuses some distance in front of the fish. Consequently there is an anterior blind spot immediately in contact with the head of the fish and this blind area is extended backwards as a sector of ever-increasing width which will only be limited by the sloping sides of the mirror. The monocular sectors form two wide areas, one on each side.

28

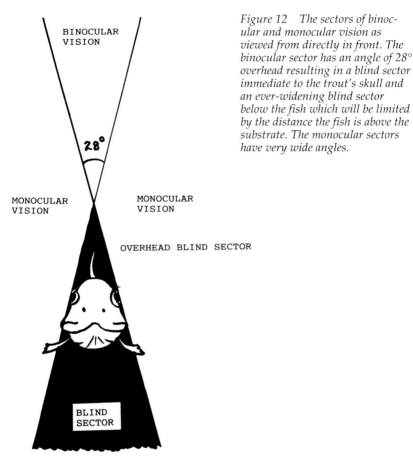

BINOCULAR
VISION

28°

MONOCULAR
VISION

MONOCULAR
VISION

OVERHEAD BLIND SECTOR

BLIND
SECTOR

*Figure 12   The sectors of binoc-
ular and monocular vision as
viewed from directly in front. The
binocular sector has an angle of 28°
overhead resulting in a blind sector
immediate to the trout's skull and
an ever-widening blind sector
below the fish which will be limited
by the distance the fish is above the
substrate. The monocular sectors
have very wide angles.*

view in each eye of 180° (figs 3 and 10) and these two fields overlap in front. Consequently, the fish's field of vision is divided into three sectors, the larger left and right sectors of monocular vision from latero-frontal to behind and a single narrow sector of binocular vision in front and overhead (figs 11 and 12). Fishing texts always describe these sections as 'arcs'. This is incorrect since an arc is defined as a portion of a curve or of the circumference of a circle. A sector is defined as a plane figure contained by two radii and the arc of a circle, a more accurate definition.

Monocular Vision

Each sector of monocular vision as seen from above the trout start at 17.5° posterior to the antero-posterior line, nose to tail (fig. 11), and therefore form right and left sectors of 162.5°. Seen from in front, the monocular sectors are slightly wider (166°) because the binocular sector overhead is only 28° instead of 35° (fig. 12).

In these monocular sectors the trout can, to quote R.J. Pumphrey, 'be assumed to have adequate vision for large objects at all distances with its unaccommodated eye' (eye unfocused). In other words the eye has a depth of field (the horizontal distance over which all objects are in focus) in these monocular zones as if focused at infinity. Consequently, focusing is not required for these monocular areas of the trout's vision and indeed such focusing is not possible because of the backward direction in which the lens travels when the retractor lentis muscle contracts as mentioned previously (fig. 1.)

Binocular Vision

Because of the disposition of its eyes the trout has binocular vision both overhead and to the front. The binocular vision to the front is a sector with an angle of 35° (plus or minus a couple of

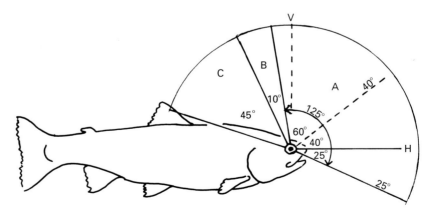

Figure 13   The various sectors of binocular vision as viewed laterally.
A is the 125° forward sector divided into a sector 25° below the horizontal which is
continuous with a sector 100° above the horizontal (H). V, vertical.
B is the sector of 10° in which focus can possibly be changed and C the 45° sector in
which the eye is always focused at infinity.

degrees) (fig. 11), while the sector directly overhead is only 28°, also plus or minus a few degrees (fig. 12). However, experiments suggest that binocular vision exists from 25° below the horizontal (as viewed from the side of the trout), to 100° above it, so forming a sector with a total angle of 125° when viewed from the side (fig. 13).

The optimum angle of most acute binocular vision is considered to be 40° from the horizontal which would normally impinge on the mirror. However, trout tend to lie with their bodies inclined slightly upwards which would bring the most acute point of binocular vision to about 45°. Since this angle is within the 48.5° angle of the window, the trout's sharpest vision would be to the anterior edge of the window where it would be most effective.

For all in-front and overhead sectors between the 25° below the horizontal to 100° there is a smaller sector immediate to the trout's surface. These sectors are 'blind spots' where the trout has neither binocular nor monocular vision. In three dimension, therefore, this blind area forms a wedge with a curved sharp upper edge and a base following the curvature of the trout's head (fig. 14). The shape of this blind spot has not previously been described in

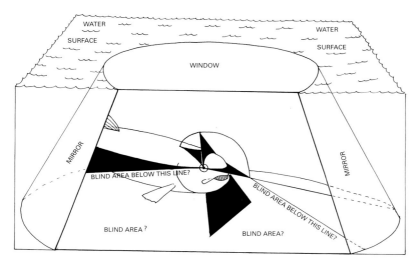

Figure 14   A three-dimensional diagram illustrating the wedge-shaped blind area immediate to the trout's 'forehead'. The front face of the mirror and window have been sliced away to reveal the interior.

fishing texts and is usually ignored, but it may account for trout rising but apparently 'missing' the fly at the last moment due to misjudging the speed at which the prey is travelling.

Immediately behind the 125° sector as viewed from the side, is a sector of 10° where a change in eye focus is considered possible. Behind this sector is a final one of some 45° where the eyes are always focused at infinity. The lower radius of this sector is virtually a backward continuation of the lower radius of the 25° below-the-horizontal sector (fig. 13). The whole of this 45° sector is not useful for binocular vision above the water since rays below 25° will impinge on the mirror; the lowest useful limit of the 45° sector for vision above water therefore follows the angle which forms the limit of the window, namely 48.5° from the vertical.

As well as the wedge-shaped blind spot already mentioned, there is another blind spot beneath and forward of the trout. The upper limit of this spot is the lower radius of the 25° below-the-horizontal sector in front of the trout. In addition, there is towards the back an ever-widening blind spot below and backwards under the horizontal line and possibly below the 48.5° angle from the vertical which defines the window (fig. 14). As already mentioned, the mirror forms a truncated cone around the fish and this combined with the blind spot is the reason why trout can be approached very closely from behind with careful wading, extreme care being needed because though the trout cannot see the fisherman, it can still detect subsurface noises or vibrations (or even heavy footfalls on the bank) by its lateral-line system.

When the eye is unaccommodated (at rest) the elliptical shape of the retina ensures that the fish is myopic (short-sighted) in its binocular sectors. To quote R.J. Pumphrey, 'the fish can see clearly with an unaccommodated eye objects just in front of its nose of the size class for which a child would have to accommodate strongly and an old man would have to use an accessory lens'. However, vision of remote objects ahead is severely limited. Pumphrey states that 'Clear vision is limited to objects at a distance of 10–20cm.' (about 4 to 12 in). 'At greater distances increased blurring of the image and decreasing angular subtense work together to prevent objects being properly seen.' In predators such as trout the contraction of the well developed retractor lentis muscle brings into focus on the temporal part of the retina remote objects in front and overhead; these objects are

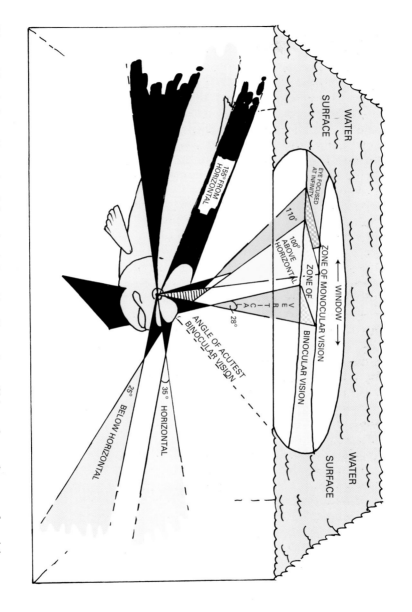

Figure 15   A three-dimensional drawing integrating the sectors of binocular and monocular vision, and the window. Possible blind spots are shown in black and the front face of the window has been sliced away to reveal the interior.

presumably located in the 125° sector of binocular vision.

Though the facts concerning the window and the various sectors of binocular and monocular vision are all important in themselves, it is necessary for the fisherman to appreciate how all these are integrated into a three-dimensional whole. Fig. 15 attempts to illustrate such an integrated picture. The sector of binocular vision intersects the window as a band which progressively widens towards the anterior. For a trout lying with his eyes situated at 15.2 cm (6 in) below the surface, the band is about 5.1 cm (2 in) wide overhead widening to about 6.4 cm (2.5 in) anteriorly. At 30 cm (1 ft) deep the figures are 12.7 cm and 16.5 cm (5 and 6.5 in) and at 60 cm (2 ft) deep, 28 and 37 cm (11 and 14.5 in) respectively. Presumably, the band widens progressively as it passes through the water surface and immediately to the front will seem to the trout to project into the air at an angle of 48.5° above the vertical, though of course the fish will see everything around it which is 10° above the horizontal.

Behind the binocular band is a rectangle of the same width where eye focus changes and behind this in turn a band widening posteriorly in which vision is at infinity. Both these bands will also widen after projecting beyond the water-air interface and the posterior part of the at-infinity sector will appear to the fish to be at an angle of 48.5° to the vertical, as for the anterior binocular sector, and everything above 10° to the horizontal will be visible. This rearward facing band has been considered a danger area for fisherman because even when the trout is focused on an object in front or overhead, the fish can see sharply anything approaching it slightly to its rear; it is in many respects like a monocular zone. This latter statement and that claiming a fish can be safely approached directly from behind, appear to be in contradiction, but the experience of fishermen confirms the latter. If a fish is high in the water, then its window is small and a close approach is possible provided one stays below 10° above the horizontal. Even if slightly above 10°, say 15°, the fisherman's image may be so distorted that the fish is not alarmed. Of course if the fisherman is only a little off centre to the rear it must be presumed he will be noticed by one of the fish's lateral monocular vision zones.

At each side of this central band of binocular vision running anterior to posterior are two lenticular-shaped areas of monocular vision. It is probably these areas which warn the fish of fishermen approaching obliquely from the rear and possibly from the side and oblique front. Where the outer boundaries of these monocular zones interact with the periphery of the window they will appear to the fish to project into the air at an angle of 48.5° to the vertical while at their inner surfaces adjacent to the central bands of the binocular, focus-change and at-infinity bands, their borders will be restricted by the expanding central binocular bands. In what ways should this knowledge of the trout's under and above-water vision inform the fisherman's approach to catching trout? Certain conclusions can be drawn and are according to John Roberts, quoting from an article by John Goddard, as follows:

1. A trout lying and feeding within, say, 18 inches (45.7 cm) or so of the surface will probably be concentrating on its binocular vision and therefore the approaching fly-fisher would probably not register unless he made any sudden movement.

2. A trout lying very close to the surface will probably be focusing below infinity, so any approaching objects, including the fly-fisherman, will be even less likely to be seen.

3. In both cases (1 and 2 above), however, accurate casting will be necessary, as the fish is unlikely to be aware of any fly drifting down to it either on or below the surface either side of a narrow arc of binocular vision.

4. A trout lying and feeding at a much deeper level is unlikely to be concentrating through its binocular vision so everything on each side of its head within the whole 160-degree arc of vision will be seen clearly at infinity.

5. Even when a trout is focusing at short range immediately ahead of it, an arc of about 45° on each side and to the rear of the fish is still focused at infinity. This is often the angle that the traditional across and upstream presentation is made, putting the fisherman in the worst possible position. Such a trout would be less likely to see the fisherman if he were either opposite it or even slightly upstream.

In the context of this book, however, a more important question than the one above is how does the trout with its various sectors of monocular and binocular vision, its window and the mirror see its prey? That is the topic of the next chapter.

Chapter 3

Triggers and Flies

The Signs that Signal Go

In recent years the dry-fly fisherman has reached a better under-standing of the factors and triggers which cause a trout to rise and take a fly. These insights are mainly due to the research carried out by fly-fishermen themselves and fishing articles and text-books written by fishermen, rather than to basic biological research on the anatomy of the fish's eye or on fish vision; the former are avidly read by fishermen while the scientific papers are not.

Nevertheless, it is pertinent to ask, with the information outlined in Chapters 1 and 2 in mind, 'How does the trout become aware of a fly floating into its window?' Before describing the sequence of events which the trout sees, it is necessary to divide the account between duns, sedges and diptera on the one hand and spinners and hatching adults on the other. The former float on the water with their bodies supported clear of the surface by their legs and feet, which do not penetrate through the surface tension film of the water. However, the feet depress the film and so give rise to localised areas where the refractive index of the surface is changed. In this text, for reasons which will become obvious later, such indentations of the surface film are called the 'footprint' on the water.

In contrast, spinners or other insects trapped in, or immediately under the surface film, or nymphs/pupa which have reached the surface, are hatching or have failed to hatch, all show their bodies and often their wings, since the latter may be spread-eagled on either side of the body or in various folded states. In addition a 'shuck' may be present, this being the remnants of the nymphal or pupal body from which the adult has just emerged. Naturally all these structures deform the surface tension film of the water to a much greater degree than the feet of the dun and form a more complex light pattern, usually with clearly revealed colours.

Ephemeroptera – the Dun

The trout is first made aware of the approach of a floating dun by the footprint in the mirror which appears to it as a series of radiating bright 'lines' or 'speckles' (fig. 16 A, B, C). At first sight the bright points will appear small and separate but as Snell's circle is approached some points fuse and so become more conspicuous; the footprint may have a prominent sparkling band next to Snell's circle just before the feet enter the window. Even the youngest fingerling must soon come to learn that this unvarying pattern is the prelude to a tasty morsel! The footprint will be most evident and be seen at the farthest distance in a smooth-flowing, unrippled stream or on a flat calm lake. However, the image will break up, be distorted and confusingly surrounded by other light sparkling figures in broken water, and by ripples, waves, wind or other forces fracturing the surface film.

Much has been made in fishing literature of the need for the artificial fly to present the quarry with this footprint as an initial trigger but the ease with which the footprint light pattern can be distorted or destroyed gives cause for question. If the water surface is disturbed by currents, underwater features, weather conditions, or other physical factors so that many sparkling light patterns occur in the mirror it might reasonably be suggested that the paramount importance given to the footprint as a significant initial trigger is overemphasised. However, we must take into

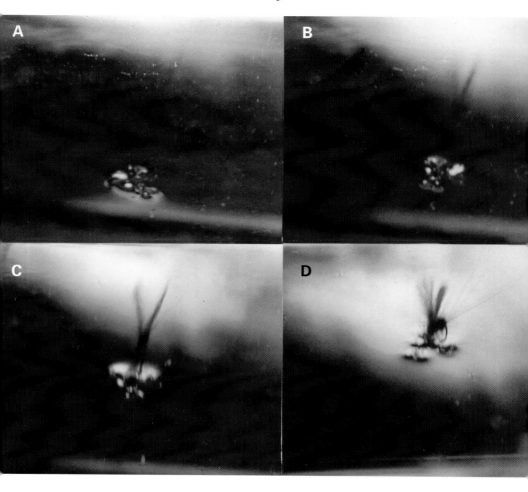

Figure 16   The sequence of signals the trout sees of the dun, when using an artificial fly.

A. The footprint in the mirror and very faint indications of the wings.

B. 'Wing flare' (dark in this case) is evident in Snell's circle.

C. The wings and the footprint are now joined and the window is evident.

D. The dun is on the edge of Snell's circle and the body and tails are clearly seen.

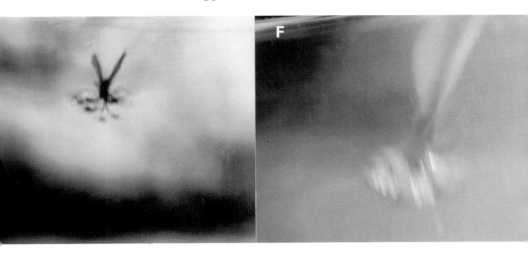

Figure 16 cont.
E. *The dun in the window with the footprint now dark and wings, body and tails are clearly seen.*

F. *'Wing flare' in Snell's circle with tinges of orange, red and blue on the white wings.*

account that the footprint is small, very characteristic in its pattern, and that trout have very sharp vision and can position themselves so as to obtain the maximum information possible concerning the object they wish to study.

It may be concluded, therefore, that provided the water surface is not totally destroyed by white water or whipped into foam, there will probably be relatively large areas of the trout's mirror which are undisturbed and within which the footprint, being small, will appear as a notable feature. This certainly seems to be the situation as experienced by many anglers, for fish are catchable with dry flies even in relatively disturbed water. Nevertheless, the greater popularity of wet flies over dry in northern parts of Great Britain, where rivers are often turbulent compared with the smooth flowing rivers of the lowland chalk streams of the south, is probably explained by the fact that the footprint is a less dominant indicator of approaching flies for trout in these faster running and more disturbed waters. Over the years northern fishermen have learned this fact and use wet flies whose underwater image is subject to less distortion.

The next 'trigger' the trout sees are the wings and not the body as one might expect. This is because the body, though clear of the water surface, does not extend into the air as much as the wings. Consequently, it is the tips of the wings which first impinge on the light rays which are 10° above the horizontal and appear to the trout uphill along the 48.5° angle from the vertical, that is close to the outer margin of Snell's circle. At this point, therefore, the fish sees simultaneously the footprint sparkles in the mirror and the ghostly, disembodied tips of the wings (fig. 16 A and B). This ghostly appearance is described as a 'flare' by Goddard and Clarke, but this is not an accurate description in all cases. The degree to which the wings 'flare', that is appear as a structure brighter than the background, seems to depend on the colour of the mirror itself. If the mirror is silvery then the flare has a pronounced whiteness which is modified by the yellows, oranges and blues of Snell's circle (fig. 16F). However, if the mirror is dark brown then the wings appear even darker than the mirror, although their edges and tips are tinged with the colours of Snell's circle. As the wings reach or enter Snell's circle they are elongated and approach the footprint (fig. 16 C and F). As already mentioned, any colouring of the wings is very probably due to the spectrum of Snell's circle, for the wings of many flies are virtually colourless. This fact poses a problem for fly tiers since most artificial wings are anything but translucent, being of feathers, hair or poly yarn, all of which are relatively solid. The wings continue to elongate until at the edge of the window they join with the body which also is now seen (fig. 16 D and E). As the fly moves towards the centre of the window the footprint changes from light sparkles to a series of dark spots (fig. 16E). At this point the tails may also be seen clearly (fig. 16 D and E).

The third signal for the trout is the colour of the body which may or may not be seen depending on the light. With intense sunlight overhead, the trout may see only a dark, colourless silhouette (fig. 17 A). However, this lack of body colour may not be inhibiting, for fly patterns with black bodies are readily taken by trout; any inhibition there might be could be overridden by the first two stimuli signalling that an acceptable food article is on the way. If the background light is less bright, or oblique, or bankside vegetation gives a greenish backcloth, then the trout may see a 'flare' of body colour (fig. 17 B), or the body colour of the fly may be perfectly clear (fig.

17 C). In the natural, the thorax region usually appears in a fairly opaque colour but the abdomen's colour may be more or less translucent. Whether this third stimulus results in a take or rejection may depend not only on the colour itself, but also the previous immediate experience of a particular fish. For example, if large dark olives have been hatching, then there may be a predisposition to take flies with only this body colour (olive green/brown) and reject other colours. Nevertheless it must be kept in mind that trout 'see' red, orange and yellow more readily than other colours and also contrasts such as black/white, red/green, yellow/black, red/white or yellow/white. Consequently, the 'wrong' body colour may be taken because it is more attractive to trout or because a particular colour or contrast is more readily visualised. These facts can be important in constructing artificial flies in colours or contrasting colours not obviously related to any natural fly.

Ephemeroptera – the Spinner

These too give a characteristic light pattern when on the water and therefore will be considered separately from hatching nymphs or pupa.

In the mirror the distinctive light outline of the spinner resembles a cross (fig. 17 D and E). Broken fringes of light surround

Figure 17
A. Dun body colour appears black though in fact it is olive.

B. 'Body flare' from a red-bodied dun pattern.

C. The true body colour of orange is evident as is the true buff wing colour.

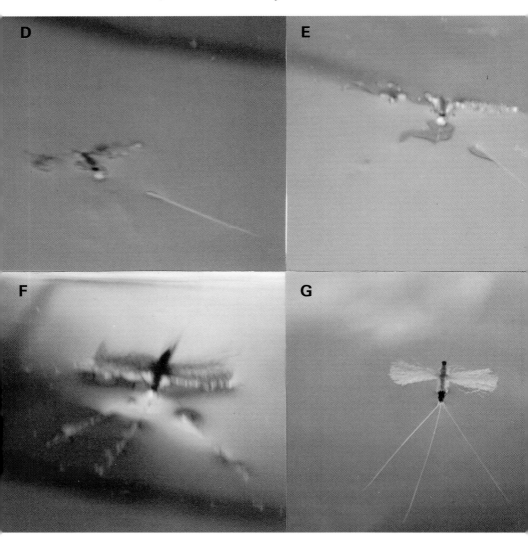

Figure 17 cont.

D. A spinner in the mirror showing the cross-light pattern, body colour and the tails.

E. This spinner is closer to the window and shows greater 'sparkle' round the wings and body; the three tails are also evident.

F. The spinner in Snell's circle showing body colour, wing sparkle and three tails.

G. A Mayfly spinner in the mirror showing clearly the body colour, wings and tails.

the body where it depresses the surface film and if the body is firmly in the mirror then the body colour is also visible (fig. 17 D and E). The wings lie flat on the water being pulled down by surface tension. They give a sparkling outline and usually show their typical form in shades of blue and off-white for most species. At all times body and wings are in contact. If the tails and legs are also in contact with the surface they form white lines or dots (fig. 17 F). As the spinner approaches the window the light fringes round the body and the wings flare up even brighter.

In the window the body appears either dark or coloured (fig. 17 G), depending on the light conditions and the wings can be seen in clear detail as bluish white or whitish grey, the colour being dependent to some extent on the colour and brightness of the sky. The two or three tails show as dark or light lines depending on background (fig. 17 G), and the legs may also be visible even if not conspicuous. With the approach of sunset and a reddening sky the appearance of the spinner in the mirror changes. The light refracted round the body and wings becomes even more obvious and changes to rainbow shades with a tendency towards orange and red. The combination of a characteristic cross light pattern and red/orange colour may account for the well known taking ability of spinner patterns in the late evening.

Diptera – the Adult

The sequence of triggers given by an adult dipteran is similar to that of the dun, that is footprint followed by wing and body (fig. 18 A, B, C, D and E). However, an important difference between the two species is that the wings of dipterans lie close to and almost parallel with the body. Consequently, the wings will not show the typical elongated, sometimes double, wing flare of the dun. Wings will only be visible when the fly and its footprint are close to or just within Snell's circle (fig. 18 D and E). Furthermore, the body may appear alongside the single faint flash of the wings (fig. 18 C and D). Since tails are not present in these flies, only the dark footprint spots, dark legs, wings and body will appear in the window, the colour of the latter being generally either black or dark green (fig 18 E and F).

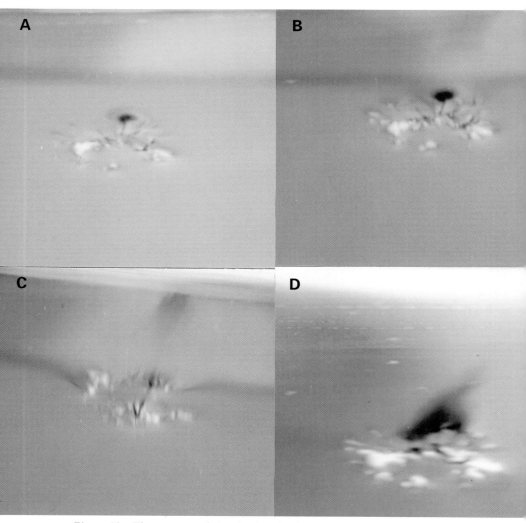

Figure 18   The sequence of signals given by dipteran patterns.

A. The footprint in the mirror.

B. The faint 'flash' of bluey-orange wings as Snell's circle is approached.

C. The wing 'flash' from the white poly yarn wings is clear. There is the suggestion of body colour below the wings and this body is attached to the legs even though the fly is not yet in Snell's circle.

D. The wings and body are united with the footprint.

Figure 18 cont.   E. The fly is just on the edge of the window and the black body colour, hook bend, legs and wings are clearly seen.

F. A Hawthorn Fly pattern just entering the window where the long back legs are very evident as are wings and legs with their dark dimples.

Trichoptera – Adult Sedges

The triggers given by sedges vary greatly because different species have different methods of egg laying, which is the reason the females approach the water surface in the first instance. For convenience the group may be divided arbitrarily into four: static floaters; moving floaters; underwater egg layers and spent sedges.

STATIC FLOATERS

These sedges rest on the surface, more or less static, and are carried along by the current. Consequently the trout initially sees the sedge as it does the dun (fig. 19 A). The footprint appears sparkling in the mirror but the body and wings are invisible, unless that is the female has her abdomen submerged, when a pronounced circle of light would be present. The sequence of events in sedges follows that of the diptera in that the footprint sparkles are not followed by typical dun-type wing flare. As the sedge approaches Snell's circle the faint image of the body is seen alongside that of the wings (fig. 19 B), and is soon attached to the footprint by the image of the legs (fig. 19 C). The wings are not seen clearly until the fly is within Snell's circle (fig. 19 D). In general, wing flare as such is hardly evident in sedges for the wings become clearly visible only as the fly leaves Snell's circle (fig. 19 E and F). There are, therefore, pronounced differences between duns and sedges which are, of course, due to the latters' wings being folded roof-like over the body, with the highest point of the roof being to the rear. However, even this high point is normally very much closer to the water surface than the more upright wings of duns and therefore it must be assumed that wing flare is not a significant signal to the trout for this species. A slight evidence of the wings may occur immediately before Snell's circle is reached (fig. 19 D) and may appear posterior to the footprint because the wings extend considerably beyond the body. Since this is unlike the situation in the dun, where the wing flare is in line with (directly above) the footprint, it may have

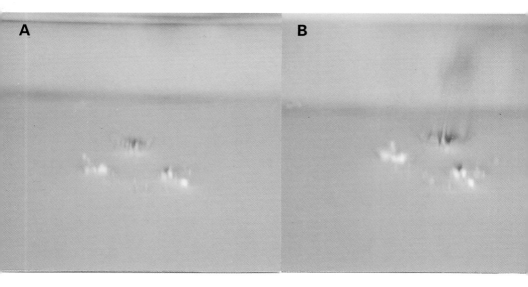

Figure 19   The sequence of signals given by a sedge pattern.
A. The footprint in the mirror.
B. The first sign of wing 'flash' as Snell's circle is approached.

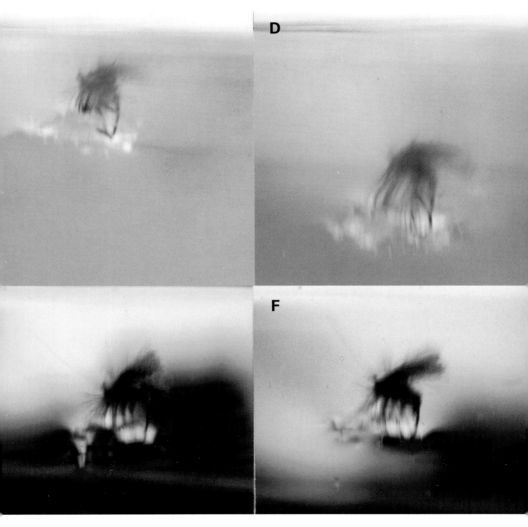

Figure 19 cont.   C. The wings low over the body and of the correct orange colour. The hook bend, legs and body are evident.

D. On the fringe of the window the body (black though actually orange), and the legs are clearly seen and the two antennae can just be seen.

E. The sedge entering the window showing the antennae, wings, body and legs.

F. Slightly further into the window where even the hackles in front of the wings can be seen along with the antennae and the bend of the hook.

some significance for trout in differentiating between dun and sedge even before the fly is sharply seen in the window.

The full shape and colour of the wings will be seen when a sedge enters the window (fig. 18 F). The roof-like shape of the wings, and their expansion rearwards beyond the body are all very characteristic and clearly distinguish the sedge from the dun. Furthermore, the wings of sedges are generally more opaque than those of the dun and more solidly coloured. Nevertheless it must be admitted that the wings of yellow mays, march browns, iron blues and some olives are quite dark and distinct but a dun's wing always has a transparency not seen in sedges. Finally, the long antennae of the sedge may be clearly seen by trout and act as a trigger (fig. 19 E and F).

MOVING SEDGES

These females run or skitter over the surface with or without their abdomen submerged. Consequently the trout is alerted by a series of moving bright spots, streaks, rings and other light forms disturbing the mirror. The abdomen below the water surface will appear double in the mirror, one image curving down and the other upwards and single in the window when the colour of the body may also be clearly seen. These images coupled to movement provide a single very strong trigger and trout will move rapidly to take the prey before it flies away. The take can be sudden and savage as many a fisherman dragging a sedge pattern across a trout's path can testify! Such trout do not wait to confirm the acceptability of the prey until it is within the window and can be checked for wing shape or colour. If many females are egg-laying, close to the water in groups with males, or sometimes even when only a solitary female or male sedge is in the air, trout may see them through their window and, using their binocular vision, launch themselves to take a fly on the wing, a thrilling sight.

UNDERWATER EGG LAYERS

Naturally, these sedges cause great disruption of the mirror as they attempt to and then break the surface film and swim under-water to the river-bed to lay their eggs. The confusing light patterns so produced have no characteristics except to be relatively large, compared to a footprint, and constantly changing.

Such fracturing of the mirror will act as a strong signal and elicit an equally strong response, such as those mentioned in the section above. The visible presence of the abdomen and wings, perhaps in bright colours, may be a strong stimulus and therefore usefully copied into some fly patterns. Despite the marked disturbance of the water surface by such underwater egg layers, it must be remembered that they generally use a structure projecting above the water surface down which they will enter the water, for example wooden piles, bridge supports and water plants. As a consequence, this group may not be as important to trout as other sedges which occupy the open water of rivers and lakes.

SPENT SEDGES
These are sedges with body and outspread wings trapped in the surface film. Such sedges give a light pattern similar to that of the spinner, namely a cross. However, the sedge has two pairs of almost equal-sized wings so that the horizontal cross-piece is broad and the vertical cross-piece will appear shortened and partly obscured by the breadth of the wings. Consequently the trout will see a broad area of bright refraction in the mirror with perhaps a hint of body and wing coloration. The sedge's more opaque wings will probably not show so conspicuously the spectrum effect when in Snell's circle or at the setting of the sun, but no evidence on this point is available at present.

Hatching Nymphs/Pupa
Only those nymphs or pupa in the surface film and actually in the process of hatching will be considered to come under the heading dry flies. Unfortunately, studies of the light patterns produced by these forms do not seem to have been made or published, and consequently it is only possible to speculate on the basis of results and facts derived from other flies. Such speculation is nevertheless useful, even if prone to the danger of error, since patterns to imitate these stages have been devised, for example Red Tag, Terry's Terror and Sparkle Duns. Further speculation may lead to improvements in these patterns or the evolution of new patterns.

If the nymph or pupal body is in the surface film, the abdomen will usually be below the surface and only the thorax and head may be above it. In the mirror the abdomen will appear twice, the real abdomen pointing down and the reflected abdomen upwards, the two joined at the surface film. In front and attached to the abdomen will be a series of sparkles round the sides of the thorax, rather in the manner of the spinner but shorter. The legs may show as light lines. The pattern in the mirror will be quite characteristic, therefore, and cannot be confused with other stages of fly life.

If hatching is occurring then the light pattern will twinkle due to the movement of the adult struggling to free itself from the nymphal or pupal shuck; this movement of the light pattern may be a strong stimulus like that of the skittering sedge. Immediately after hatching, with the adult still in contact with the shuck as it expands its wings and dries out, there will be a change in the refractive index of the shuck which should now be translucent. This shuck should give a broad light pattern like a spinner's wing when in the mirror, or a spectral pattern in Snell's circle or evening sunset.

As the adult on its shuck floats towards the window, wing flare should be observed in the dun, even though no footprint is evident. In the window both the shuck and the adult will be observed, though the translucent shuck may obscure the trout's accurate observation of colour, shape, etc. of the adult or distort its image. The large size of the combined shuck and adult may be strongly stimulating, a choice morsel which a trout knows by experience may be about to leave at any moment and so a quick response is needed. Since most patterns of hatching adult flies have red, orange, or combined red/orange 'tails' to simulate the shuck, this may be the normal appearance of these structures, although the sparkle duns with their reflective translucent materials, such as Krystal Flash, also elicit a good response; perhaps these latter represent the shuck after the adult has emerged.

Size
Consideration of light patterns, movement and colour ignores another possible trigger which will stimulate trout to rise and take, namely that of size. Even if all the other essential factors are present, the trout may not respond because the size of the pattern being fished is not correct. Artificial patterns are often larger than the naturals they attempt to imitate, even when tied on small

hooks, say 16 or 18. Though in animal behaviour studies stimuli larger than the natural, so-called 'super stimuli', elicit a greater response than the normal, we do not know if this is the case with artificial flies and trout. Experience confirms that a smaller or larger pattern may take fish when a different size of the very same pattern does not. This is a factor which can only be corrected at the stream side, having previously been anticipated at the bench.

In summary, therefore, it may be stated that the important triggers which stimulate predation by trout and the sequence of those triggers which the fly tier must incorporate into his patterns are, in order of significance, as follows:

Dun – footprint, wing flash, colour of body and wing.

Spinner – cross light pattern, wings clearly defined, body and wing colour, spread legs.

Sedge (static type) – footprint, wing and body colour.

Sedge (moving type) – movement of footprint, wing and body colour.

Underwater egg layers – movement of large but changing light pattern, abdomen below the water, accurate representation of swimming female as to body and wing size, shape and colour.

Spent sedges – bloated cross shape light pattern, colour of body and wings.

Hatching nymphs/pupa – light pattern of abdomen and/or thorax, wing flash, shuck shape and colour, adult size, shape and colour.

It is well within the fly tier's capabilities to imitate these light patterns, so ensuring the correct signals are given to the trout in the mirror and the window. However, the movement of the natural fly is another factor which may act as a stimulus to the trout's predatory behaviour and is almost impossible to 'build' into a fly. The Janus fly is claimed to move on the water as a result of the rear upright tail and the double winging on traditional patterns, and the new patterns yet to be described in this book may move in response to the fingers of a breeze caressing them, but these are chance events, negated by still days and still water. The good response that is dependent on the dragging of a sedge pattern across the nose of a trout is familiar to all dry-fly men and is a controlled event, but drag is generally considered to be detrimental to the fishing of most dry flies. Movement of the fly, whether it be the dipping on and off the water in egg-laying or the skittering of sedges and mayflies, would appear to be characteristics of *natural* flies which are ever to remain beyond the bounds of fly tying as an art.

Chapter 4

Patterns of Development

The history of dry-fly patterns has been one of continuous development. Each generation of fishermen has attempted to improve the effectiveness of old patterns or evolve entirely new designs in the light of their current knowledge concerning the biology of their quarry and the availability of new materials, mostly man-made. In recent years the proliferation of fishing journals and books has led to the rapid dissemination of variations on existing patterns of both wet and dry flies, and to the origin of many new and highly original patterns which are sometimes specifically targeted to certain situations or fish.

The 'standard' or 'classical' dry-fly pattern for the dun is comprised of a good quality stiff hackle behind the eye, wings or suggestions of them and a stiff bunch of tail fibres. On the water the fly rests on the forward hackles and the tail fibres, so that if properly tied and proportioned, the hook is clear of the water (fig. 20 A). However, if the hackles are not stiff enough, the body rests unnaturally on or in the surface film. Conversely, if the hackles are too firm they penetrate the surface film and appear as double structures in the reflecting mirror and as a number of most unnatural dark fibres in the window. Unfortunately the standard pattern, even when correctly tied, does not give the correct light triggers. The footprint is too localised near the eye and the tail gives a light pattern not shown by the natural fly, which keeps its tails free of the water. Even palmered and parachute flies fail to give the correct triggers in the right sequence. Nevertheless, such patterns catch fish, even though I suspect it is not as many as they would, perhaps, if they gave rise to the right stimulatory signals in the correct sequence. In my experience these patterns are most successful within the first few casts when they ride high, but once the fly settles into the water they lose part of their effectiveness.

Of the dry-fly developments in recent years the Clarke and Goddard USD Paraduns (fig. 20 B) most nearly supply all the triggers to which a trout responds: footprint, wing flash from stiff cut wings, body above the surface due to a parachute hackle and

Figure 20

A. *A fly tied in the classical manner with a front hackle and tail keeping the barb above the surface.*

B. *A USD Paradun with a parachute hackle below and wings cut from near the tips of a hackle; due to the USD form the body and barb are well above the surface and the fly is very realistic in appearance.*

Figure 20 cont.
C. A Marinaro-type Thorax Dun with a bunch of tail fibres, two hackles in an
X-formation and poly yarn wings; the barb is well above the surface.

correct body colour. Such being the case it is surprising that the pattern has not made all other dun patterns redundant. Sadly it is a fact that the pattern has gone into decline and generally does not figure as it once did in the majority of fishing catalogues or journals.

The reasons for this decline are not difficult to discover. The USD Paradun is time-consuming to tie, requires dexterity, experience and skill not always abundant among amateur fly tiers, and if not well-made does not land upright on the water. The tying-in of the cut wings and the imposition of an outward curve to them is daunting in itself, but added to this is the tying of the parachute hackle, another very tricky manoeuvre and the trying fact that the hook must be reversed in the vice at one stage. To quote Clarke and Goddard, 'It is worth stating at the onset that these flies are not the easiest of patterns to tie, and that the dresser needs all the basic skills of the trade in order to produce a good finished article. It may be most profitable in terms of time and effort, therefore, to reserve them for very special or difficult trout.'

Figure 20 cont.
D. A Footprint Fly with the hackle wound Footprint fashion, with two pairs of Betts'
tailing fibres and poly yarn wings; the barb is just above the surface.

This statement is certainly a douche of cold water and human nature being what it is, it probably elicits the response 'thanks but no thanks'. Fishermen do not want to tie flies which are so difficult that they must be kept for special occasions. Amateur fly tiers require a better return for their efforts, a fly for all seasons is more their motto. Furthermore there is the suspicion amongst fishermen that USD flies do not hook as well as RWU flies (right way up), though it would be hard to prove this suspicion scientifically. Hooking with USD flies is usually through the upper lip, whereas with RWU patterns it can be almost anywhere from the angle of the jaw and the lips to as far back as the tongue. Whatever the truth of the matter, this suspicion remains and is a further deterrent to fishermen adopting the USD Paradun as his standard dun pattern. In many ways this is a great pity, for the USD Paradun was developed on the basis of sound observations and with a scientific approach; it was, and still is, a very elegant solution to a difficult problem, but its inherent drawbacks have overshadowed its obvious qualities.

Previous to Clarke and Goddard's efforts, Vincent Marinaro in the 1970s devised the Thorax series of flies. These flies are characterised by wings cut from broad-neck hackles and positioned in the centre of the hook, two sets of tail fibres widely spaced to act as balancers and two hackles wound fore and aft of the wings in an X-pattern, the smaller hackle facing down and forward and the larger down and backwards. The result is a well-balanced fly which rides high on the water with the hook above the surface (fig. 20 C). Consequently, it should give the correct series of light stimuli, namely footprint and wing flash as well as the appropriate body colour. The Thorax Fly would appear to have all the characteristics necessary for success with fishermen, but despite Marinaro's books *A Modern Dry Fly Code* and *In the Ring of the Rise*, this system fly has apparently not caught on with fishermen.

I willingly confess that Marinaro and his Thorax Flies were unknown to me until I read John Roberts' *To Rise a Trout*, a comprehensive and discerning text. Perhaps my previous ignorance of the Marinaro system is still widespread amongst the fishing fraternity or the attractions of the tying are not appreciated. Whatever the situation, it was becoming aware of the Thorax Flies which transferred my vain attempts to simplify and make 'cost-effective' the USD Paradun pattern into more fruitful channels.

The key factor which impressed me about the Thorax Fly pattern was the X-formation of the two hackles which had all the advantages of the parachute hackles of the USD Paraduns but none of its drawbacks. The whole fly and its hackling could be carried out with the hook in its normal position, though the production and tying-in of the cut wings was not easy, or so I found, but they could be replaced easily by polypropylene yarn (poly yarn). With this pattern, the hook rides clear of the water, without having to rely on tail fibres touching the water surface and giving an unnatural light pattern.

The Footprint Fly system described in the next chapter is a direct descendant of the Thorax Fly system of Vincent Marinaro and I am happy to acknowledge its parentage. Though my experience was that the Marinaro flies were excellent, sitting high on the water and certainly attracting fish, I believed they could be improved, especially with regard to ease of tying. The Footprint

Fly system differs in certain essential aspects from the Thorax type. First, the formation of wings and their tying-in has been simplified to give a more constantly acceptable result since it uses a material, poly yarn, which is more amenable to clumsy fingers! Second, the hackling has also been simplified by using a single hackle and hence requires a single tying-in and a saving of expensive hackles. Though the Thorax Fly system normally uses two hackles, it has to be said that Marinaro does mention the possibility of using only one hackle, if long enough. Nevertheless the Footprint method of hackling is essentially different from Marinaro's and is, I believe, unique because it combines the advantages of both the X-pattern of the Thorax Flies and of parachute hackling. Third, the tails have been modified by use of Betts' tailing fibres or stripped hackles which give a much more natural appearance to the rear of the fly than do two large bunches of fibres. Finally, the tying uses new materials, such as poly yarn, Benecchi New Dub and Krystal Flash for the bodies; some of these materials were not available to Marinaro, of course (fig. 20D).

In conclusion, therefore, it may be said that the principals for the development of the Footprint Fly system were as follows:

1. The pattern had to incorporate a method of hackling which would raise the barb clear of the surface and also give the correct 'footprint'.
2. The pattern had to have paired wings which were easy to make and tie-in and which would give wing flare in the mirror and be clearly visible in the window.
3. The pattern had to have the proper aerodynamics which would ensure it alighted correctly on the water in virtually all circumstances. This involved the incorporation of various types of stabilisers in some patterns.
4. The pattern had to be one even the inexperienced fly tier could master and consistently produce flies of the required quality in the required quantity.
5. The pattern had to be a system fly which could be modified as to body and wing colour to imitate the majority of ephemerid duns, adult sedges, dipteran adults and with the potential for providing spinner patterns also.

6. The pattern had to have the hook RWU. The pattern had to be capable of being tied down to at least size 18 hooks by fly tiers of average ability.

How these requirements were fulfilled is detailed in Chapter 5.

Chapter 5

The Basic Principles of the Footprint Fly System (Ephemeroptera)

A. The RWU Dun with Two Wings – Tying Sequence

1.   The hook of choice is size 12 to 18. I generally use a size 16 for all patterns except Mayflies, for which I use size 14 and rarely size 12. With size 14, and particularly size 12, it is difficult to find hackles which are stiff enough to support the heavier hook, but with careful positioning a smaller hackle than suggested for other sizes can be used (see 12 below).

2.   Choose an appropriate coloured silk and wind it down to slightly beyond the bend and then back to the bend. Form a pad of silk for the tails (fig. 21 A).

3.   Using Betts' tailing fibres tie in four fibres as two pairs immediately behind the pad so that each pair points slightly upwards. The two pairs of tails must form a wide angle between them, about 90°, and this is most easily done if each pair of tails is tied-in separately. Alternatively, a single pair of stripped hackles can be used with the natural curve of the hackle pointing upwards;

the pair of stripped hackles fibres act like the two pair of Betts' tailing fibres (fig. 21 A and B). If difficulty is experienced in tying-in the two pairs of Betts' tailing fibres or in keeping the stripped hackles curving upwards when tying, place a spot of Floo Gloo on the silk, let it become tacky and then place the fibres or hackle on it. Trim the tails to length, keeping them fairly long. Keep the two 'tails' well apart with a drop of Floo Gloo or varnish (fig. 21 B and C).

These tail fibres are essential features of this fly pattern as they ensure the fly alights upright consistently. If the fly tier finds his flies with two pairs of Betts' fibres or a single pair of stripped hackles do not consistently land upright when tested or in use, then he should increase the number of Betts' fibres to three or more each side and again establish a large angle between the bunches. With an increasing number of tailing fibres the fly will descend more and more slowly. With eight or ten tailing fibres it is unnecessary to divide them into two bunches, descent will be measured, and the fly will alight gently on the water. In my view it is best to limit the number of Betts' fibres or hackles to the lowest number which consistently gives upright landing.

4.   Either use the tying silk to form a body if you wish it to be very slim (fig. 21 D and E) or tie in a length of poly yarn or Benecchi dubbing on a string of the appropriate colour for a more substantial body and thorax. If a ribbing is desired, tie it in at this point. Though I rarely use ribbing, my preferred material is Krystal Flash, either yellow or pearl. Metallic ribbing should be avoided as it adds unnecessary weight which the hackles must support. In my experience Benecchi dubbing is best since it also provides ridges on which the hackle winding for the feet can 'catch' (see 11 and 12 below).

5.   If body material and/or ribbing are being used, take to the eye, tie off and trim off the excess.

6.   Cut a short strip of poly yarn of a colour appropriate to the fly species being copied. Avoid white which is too stark and looks unnatural. My preferred colours are beige and grey. A piece of yarn about 2.5 cm long is about right and the piece should not be too thick. The wings are placed just anterior to the middle of the body and tied in using a figure-of-eight tying. A drop of Floo Gloo is placed in the centre to fix them to the body. Do not use too thick

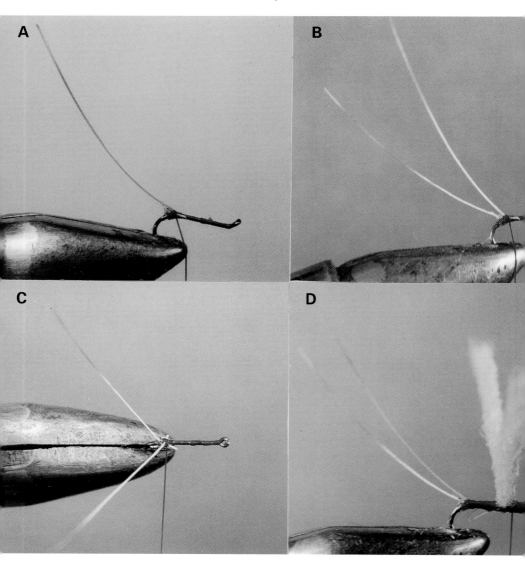

Figure 21   Footprint Fly. Ephemeroptera.
A, B, C. Tying in of stripped hackle tails.
D. Wings and body tied in.

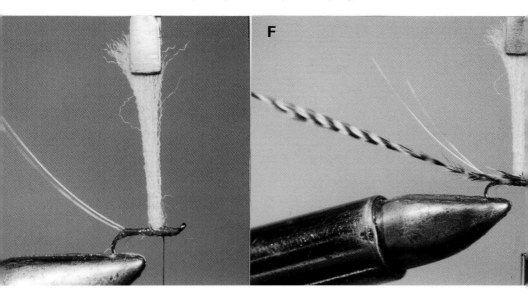

Figure 21 cont.
E. Wings in a gallows tool.
F. Hackle tied in.

a piece of poly yarn which will appear unnatural (see 15 below for the method of avoiding this situation).

7.   Place the wings in a gallows tool (fig. 21 E).

8.   Choose a hackle by spreading its fibres at a right-angle to the shaft and measuring it against the hook by placing the shaft in line with the wings. The hackle fibres should be long enough to project just beyond the hook bend. Hackle fibres about 5–6 mm long are about right for a size 16 hook. Tie in the hackle immediately in front of the wings with the butt facing towards the eye and the hackle curvature upwards. Trim off the butt (fig. 21 F). I confine myself to good quality grizzle or white hackles and of the two I prefer grizzle, which I feel more nearly resembles the appearance of the legs of most insects. I believe other more solidly-coloured hackles show up too starkly in the fish's window and I suspect that these dark 'legs' or too many visible 'legs' may be a deterrent to fish taking the fly.

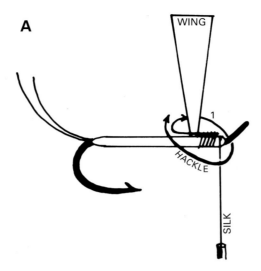

Figure 22   Footprint Fly. Ephemeroptera. Method of winding the hackle Footprint fashion.

A. Anterior winding to form front 'feet'.

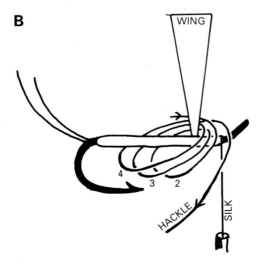

B. Posterior winding to form hind 'feet'; three turns are shown but small hooks may only require two

9.   Wind the silk halfway to the eye and leave the bobbin hanging (fig. 21 F).

10. Using hackle pliers wind the hackle round the back of the wings, then forward under the hook shaft, round the tying silk and back to the rear of the wings again, so forming the front 'feet' (fig. 22 A).

11. Take the hackle round the front of the base of the wings again and then backwards underneath towards the barb, making sure the hackles lie at an oblique angle. Repeat this two or three times, ensuring that each turn lies behind the previous one. Two turns should be sufficient for size 16 and 18 hooks (fig. 22 B). I suspect it is best to have the fewest hackles possible since the footprint will then more nearly resemble the natural insect. The last turn should ensure the hackle fibres project beyond the hook bend. (With larger hooks, 12 and 14, make sure the wings are tied in halfway or only slightly in front of halfway along the hook shank so that the hackle fibres project at least to the hook bend. Hackle fibres about 7–8 mm should suffice and support the barb above the water even if they do not project beyond the barb itself. If this tactic does not succeed then it may be necessary to use a longer hackle and more turns to provide more 'feet'.) Bring the hackle round the front of the wing again and let the hackle pliers hang down on the near side of the hook, close to the eye (fig. 23 A).

12. Take the tying silk round the back of the hackle and using a half-hitch tool tie it in; repeat this three times making sure not to trap any hackle fibres pointing forwards (fig. 23 B). The latter is best accomplished by making sure the half-hitch tool and the tying silk are in line with the hook length.

13. Trim off the hackle and if you wish add some more silk to the head using the half-hitch tool. Cut the silk.

14. Trim off the hackle fibres above the horizontal so as to reveal the body colour (fig. 23 B). This is relatively easy if the wing is left in the gallows tool but moved backwards, forwards and sideways with the finger as necessary. This is not an essential step but it is my unsupported impression that fish are 'put off' by seeing the hackles fibres round the wings. If these hackles are left on, the fly will float down more slowly and land upright more consistently.

These above-the-horizontal hackle fibres are retained in Marinaro's Thorax Dun pattern but he states that the hackle should 'supplement and confirm' the wing colour, which means that wing and hackle should be of the same colour. This observation of Marinaro supports the author's supposition that the upper hackles fibres should normally be removed since the Footprint pattern as given here uses grizzle or white hackles exclusively whatever the variant. There is probably scope for experimentation here to prove whether or not using hackles which match the wing colour would improve the attractiveness of the fly. Hackles of white, buff or grey would cover most species of ephemerids. If the fly tier wishes to leave the above-the-horizontal fibres on, they may be stained with Studio Colour pens (Magic Marker brand), to match the wing colour. This is a rather tedious process to do after the fly is tied but can be successfully accomplished with care and putting a slip of paper between hackles and wing. Studio Colours are resistant to most silicone fly flotants, but test first.

15. Trim the wings to length depending on the size of hook; anything between 0.5 cm and 1 cm is usually about right. This is

Fig. 23   Footprint Fly. Ephemeroptera.
A. Immediately after winding on the hackle.
B. The above-the-horizontal hackles have been removed.

Figure 23 cont.
C. *and* D. *The finished fly from the side and rear.*
E. *and* F. *The general ephemerid Footprint Fly pattern floating on a water surface.*

best done while the wings are still held in the gallows tool. Place a spot of Floo Gloo between and round the wings to ensure they stay apart and the hackle is locked in. Round off the tips of the wings.

Thick poly wings lack transparency and being solid give a very obvious and pronounced wing flash. I have the impression that this may prevent fish from taking, even when their initial interest has been captured by the footprint on the water. Larger wings need stiffening with Floo Gloo over the basal region of each wing and all wings should be stiffened by being stroked between the thumb and forefinger on which a drop of Floo Gloo has been spread. Before the glue sets, the wings should be combed with a needle to spread their tips and make them less dense.

16. Place a spot of Floo Gloo on the head.
17. Treat the fly with silicone floatant and allow to dry.
18. When viewed from below the hackle should form a series of radiating spokes. Any hackle fibres projecting directly down-wards should be removed. The fly should sit firmly on the tying bench, level or with the head slightly tilted downwards and the barb should be clear of the surface (fig. 23 C). From the front or back the fly should sit level (fig. 23 D); if not either spread the hackle fibres or remove the offending ones. On the water the fly should sit more or less level with the hook clear of the surface (fig. 23 E and F).

B. The RWU Dun with One Wing – Tying Sequence

1. Follow stages 1 to 4 of the dun with two wings.
2. Only one wing can be used, since when at rest on the water the dun's wings are often virtually together and from certain angles may appear as a single structure. Form a wing by cutting a length of poly yarn of the appropriate colour for the species of dun being imitated, then tie in the yarn starting a little way behind the eye and continue winding the silk backwards to just before halfway, so forming a thorax.
3. Tie in a hackle immediately in front of the wing with the butt facing along the length of the hook towards the eye, and the hackle curvature upwards. Trim off the butt.
4. Wind the silk halfway to the eye and leave the bobbin hanging.
5. Hold the wing taut and upright in a gallows tool.

6.   Wind the hackle as in stages 11 to 15 of the dun with two wings pattern.

7.   Cut the wing to between 0.5–1 cm depending on the size of hook. Shape the tip of the wing to give a rounded outline and place a drop of Floo Gloo round the base of the wing to lock in the hackle.

8.   Follow stages 17 to 19 in the schedule for the dun with two wings.

C. Egg-laying Dun – Tying Sequence

This pattern is tied as for the dun with two wings except for two essential differences, namely:

1.   Take the silk about a third of the way round the bend of the hook and tie in a thin strand of green poly yarn. Form a small egg ball with the green yarn. Tie off and trim. An alternative is to use yellow or mother-of-pearl Krystal Flash to form the egg ball (fig. 24).

2.   When tying in the wings place them slightly forwards of the normal position for the dun pattern, or leave the wings in their usual position but use a hackle shorter than normal, i.e. one which does not extend beyond the hook bend. Reverse the normal winding sequence, that is wind the hackle as described for the dun but form the front 'legs' with two turns underneath to the front and only one underneath to the rear. These methods should result in the bend of the hook dipping into the water, where the trout should see the abdomen and egg ball (fig. 24). Check that the fly does sit 'tail down' by placing it on the water after treating the hackles to float but not the egg ball. If the fly does not sit tail down, move the wings slightly further forward in the next tying.

D. Spinner – Tying Sequence

1.   Hook size 12 to 18 depending on species to be imitated, 12–14 for large flies such as mayflies, large green dun or march brown, 16–18 for small to medium flies such as olives, spurwings, BWO, or iron blue.

2.   Place the hook in the vice RWU.

3.   Use a colour of silk appropriate to the species being imitated and wind it down the shank and part way round the bend. Return the silk to the end of the shank, form a small pad and tie in two

or three Betts' tailing fibres or two stripped hackles. The balancing properties of the tails are not so important in this pattern, since it does not matter which way up the spinner lands, though this will normally be barb down. Make sure the tails are wide apart and in line with the shank of the hook, so that they will lie on the water surface when cast (fig. 25).

4.   Tie in Benecchi dubbing of the appropriate colour. At this point there are two possible patterns, those with a body and thorax of a single colour (monocolour body) and those with a light-coloured body and a dark thorax (bicolour body). (See Chapter 7 under Spinner patterns.) The reason for the bicolour body is that many of the smaller species, but not all, have a thorax which is darker than the abdomen. e.g. large, dark and medium olives, BWO and iron blue. Others such as large and small spurwing, pale watery and pale evening spinners have a virtu-ally uniform body colour, usually yellowish or whitish. In my experience both bicolour and monocolour forms seem to work equally well. Poly yarn can be used as an alternative for the body.

5.   Take the silk back from the eye a short distance and tie in poly yarn wings using a figure-of-eight tying. White yarn is appro-priate for spinners since most spinner wings are translucent. Take the silk to the eye, form a head and tie off (fig. 25).

6.   Place a drop of Floo Gloo on the centre of the wing tying and spread a little up each wing with a needle. This strengthens the roots of the wings but be sure to confine the glue to the wing base.

7.   Trim the wings so that each is about the same length as the body but be sure that they are not so long as to catch in the hook bend. Round the ends and spread the fibres by combing with a needle; the wings should be semi-translucent. Stiffen the wings by stroking them with Floo Gloo spread between finger and thumb but make sure the fibres do not bunch together again; if they do, then comb them again before the glue dries. A correct light signal will not occur unless the wings are separated into thin fibres, so combing is very important for the success of this pattern.

8.   Treat with floatant. When placed on the water the spinner should lie with the tails, wings and body on or slightly in, the surface film. Legs do not seem necessary in my experience, though doubtless trout see these in the natural. Perhaps the reason that the absence of the dark lines of the legs are not missed by the trout is because of the characteristic large sparkling cross

Figure 24   Egg-laying Mayfly; only one pair of tails is shown but two pairs are preferable.

the pattern produces. However, if the fisherman requires them, then a hackle can be tied in after the wings. Tie in the hackle in front of the wing, and take it in a figure-of-eight pattern round the wings. Tie off and trim away all hackle fibres except those projecting laterally.

TESTING THE FLY
The procedure below applies to both the dun with two wings and with one.
1.   Drop the fly from about 4–5 ft above a carpet. It should float down with the wing(s) uppermost. It may rotate a little but provided the rotation is slow, it does not seem to matter when actually casting at the waterside. The fly should bounce on the carpet and stay upright. The single wing pattern does not land upright as consistently as the two-winged variety if both have the same number of Betts' tailing or hackle tails. Consequently, it may prove necessary to increase the number of tails with the single wing variety. If either pattern repeatedly lands on its side

71

Figure 25   Footprint Flies. Ephemeroptera. Yellow/black Mayfly spinner.

or upside down, this may be due to any one or more of the following factors:

- The wing(s) is (are) too long.
- If the wing(s) seem of the right length, then move the tails further apart and reglue. As stated previously, these tails act as balancers and also 'push' the fly upright if it lands sideways. Increase the number of tail fibres in subsequent tyings if necessary.
- Some hackle fibres are projecting vertically downwards. Remove them.

2.   Place the fly on the water surface in a glass bowl. It should ride high but slightly head down and the barb should be clear of the surface (fig. 23 E and F). Look at the fly from below and it should show the starburst footprint but no hackles should project through the surface film. If the fly persistently sits or settles down with the barb below the water level, then the wing is too near the eye. Winding a hackle round a wing too far forward results in the radiating hackles not projecting backwards enough to

support the barb above the water. The propensity for hackles wound round wings close to the eye leading to barbs below the water, can be used to advantage in tying patterns to represent egg-laying female, as will be detailed in another pattern.

TIPS ON USING FOOTPRINT FLIES

After a catch the fly should be dried with amidou and then treated with floatant or drying powder. If the fly does not continue to land upright after the first few casts then return it to the fly box for a further liquid floatant treatment at home and replace it with a new fly. I always carry a bottle of Floo Gloo when fishing so that if the wings have become ragged and/or soft I can stroke them again with Floo Gloo and allow them to dry.

The colours I use for dun bodies are yellow, orange, red, buff (olive), grey or insect green. Combinations of colours are also useful, the first mentioned of the following pairs being at the tail, red/grey, black/yellow, black/white, yellow/orange, green/yellow and red/green. Though some of these combinations do not occur in nature, the reason for choosing such combinations rests entirely on the known ability of trout to be aware of contrasts and their sensitivity to certain colours as noted in earlier chapters.

Chapter 6

The Basic Principles of the Footprint Fly System (Trichoptera and Diptera)

Trichoptera

A. Floating Adult Sedge
1.   Hook size 14 or 16.
2.   Select a silk appropriate to the body colour of the species being imitated. Start the silk at the eye and take it halfway round the bend and then back to the straight part of the shank.
3.   Tie in a piece of Benecchi dub or poly yarn of the appropriate colour (fig. 26 A).
4.   Wind the silk to slightly forward of halfway along the shank.
5.   Tie in a stripped hackle with the butt facing forward and nearly touching the eye (fig. 26 A). Wind the silk over the butt towards the eye to form a thicker thorax. This stripped hackle acts as a post round which the hackle for the legs will eventually be wound and will hereafter be called a hackle post. Place the stripped hackle in a gallows tool so that it is taut.
6.   Wind on the dub or yarn ensuring it is close to the hackle post

at the back (so that the post sits upright) and take one turn of dubbing in front of the post and tie off. Be sure to leave enough space between the end of the dubbing and the eye for the wings and antennae to be tied in (fig. 26 B).

7. Form a pair of wings by folding a piece of poly yarn of the appropriate colour into a V. Place one arm of the V each side of the hackle post and the apex of the V between hackle post and eye. Tie in the butt of the V just behind the eye and wind the silk backwards towards the hackle post, so forming a thorax. As a result the wings come to lie along the upper sides of the body. Trim off any excess yarn short of the eye (fig. 26 B).

A single wing pattern is an alternative. A single piece of poly yarn is tied in close to the hackle post, the longer posterior end forming the wing and the shorter anterior part a thorax. Silk is wound close to the eye to cover the poly yarn which should be

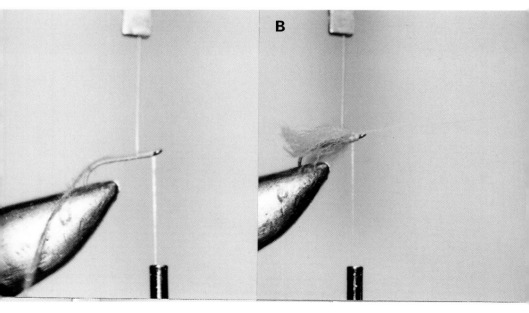

Figure 26   Footprint Fly. Trichoptera.
A. Benecchi dub tied in at tail and hackle post in position.
B. The two poly yarn wings tied in.

Figure 26 cont.
C. The wings held horizontally over the eye and the grizzle hackle tied in.

D. The hackle has been wound on and the rear above-the-horizontal fibres removed.

E. The finished fly in the vice.

F. The sedge floating on a water surface.

cut off short of the eye to leave enough space for tying in the antennae.

8.   Tie in two pairs of Betts' tailing fibres immediately behind the eye to form antennae, which should be about 0.75 in long. They must point upwards and form a wide angle. This is most easily accomplished if each pair of fibres is tied in separately and at an acute angle to the direction of the shaft of the hook. These antennae are very important as they ensure that the fly alights the right way up the majority of the time, i.e. they are the equal to the tail fibres of the dun (fig. 26 E, F).

9.   Fold the wing(s) forwards out of the way and keep it (them) there (fig. 26 C). This latter operation can be accomplished by placing the wing(s) in hackle pliers and holding the pliers horizontally with a spring or elastic band attached to some convenient vertical body at the right level and distance. I use the arm of a fitment whose original purpose was to hold a magnifying lens in front of the fly; the stem of the vice runs through a block which contains another hole for the fitment arm itself, which can be adjusted for length.

10. Tie in a hackle in front of the hackle post and then behind it (fig. 26 C). Trim off the excess, wind the silk back to halfway between eye and post and allow to hang.

11. Using hackle pliers, wind the hackle as for the dun using the hackle post in place of the wings of the latter pattern. One forward turn and two behind is usually sufficient (fig. 26 D).

12. Let the hackle pliers hang down on the nearside of the fly between hackle post and wing base (fig. 24 D). Release the wings from the pliers and fold them to the rear, one each side of the hackle post. I simply reverse the arm with attached hackle pliers which previously held the wings out of the way anteriorily so that it is now directly behind the bend of the hook. With the single wing simply pull it back to one side of the hackle post.

13. Tie off the hackle by taking the silk behind the hackle and using a hitch tool make a half-hitch behind the eye but in front of the antennae; be careful not to trap the latter and flatten them. Repeat this three times.

14. Trim off the hackle fibres immediately behind the post so as to allow the wings to sit properly. Leave the other above-the-horizontal hackle fibres as these, along with the antennae, help

the fly to float down RWU. These above-the-horizontal fibres may be coloured to match the wing using Studio Colours (Speedry Magic Marker). Apply a drop of Floo Gloo to the base of the stripped hackle post to lock in the hackle.

15. Apply a drop of Floo Gloo to the hackle post where it projects from between the wings; this holds the wings in position (fig. 26 E). Maintain the wings in a backwards direction parallel to the hook shank using hackle pliers until the glue sets. If the wings will not lie flat, lift the wings and place a drop of Uhu glue under them and replace them in the hackle pliers again until dry. For the single wing pattern, cut off the hackle post close to the body, add a drop of Floo Gloo and hold the wing down and backwards until set in the same way as for paired wings.

16. Trim off the hackle post for the paired wing pattern.

17. Place a drop of Floo Gloo on the head.

18. Stiffen and spread the wings a little by rubbing a drop of Floo Gloo between forefinger and thumb and stroking each wing in turn in a backwards direction between them. Trim wings at an angle which will give a V-shape when they are viewed from above (fig. 26 E). The wings must be spaced apart at an angle of about 45° to allow the air to pass between them. If the wings form a solid 'roof' the fly will persistently turn so that it lands upside-down.

TESTING THE FLY

This pattern may not land RWU as consistently as the dun pattern because of the sloping position of the wings. The fly should float down wings uppermost when dropped from 4 or 5 feet but it may rotate a little. However, the antennae and hackles do stabilise the pattern to a large degree and the former must be positioned wide apart so as to tip the fly upright if it tends to land on its side. The antennae must be at an upward angle to preclude them lying in the water. A wide angle between the antennae is also needed if difficulty in tying the fly to a tippet is to be avoided. The fly should ride high on the water with the barb in the air (fig. 26 F).

B. Spent Sedge – Tying Sequence

1. Hook size 14 to 18.
2. Use silk of a colour appropriate to the species being imitated.

Wind the silk to halfway round the bend and back to the start of the bend.

3.   Tie in poly yarn or Benecchi dub of the appropriate body colour and take the silk to the eye.

4.   Wind on the yarn or dub to the eye, tie off and trim.

5.   Take the silk back to just forward of halfway along the shank. Tie in a short length of poly yarn of the appropriate colour so that it lies at an angle to the hook shaft, the longer part of the yarn at the front to form the front wing. Repeat this with a second piece of yarn so as to form an X. Bind the two pairs of wings with a figure-of-eight tying and place a drop of Floo Gloo in the centre of the X to lock the wings to the body (fig. 27).

Figure 27   Spent Sedge. Only one pair of antennae is shown but two pairs are preferred.

6.   Tie in a pair of Betts' tailing fibres at each side of the eye to form antennae. Keep them more or less in line with the hook shank.

7. Finish off the head using the hitch tool.
8. Shape the wings ensuring the hind pair are shorter than the front ones. The wing tips should be rounded with the front edge of each wing longer than the back edge. Smear the wings with Floo Gloo to stiffen them slightly but be sure they are not too thick by combing them with a needle before they set (fig. 27).

It does not matter which way up this pattern lands provided the wings are in contact with the water surface. Trout prefer the small size 16 or 18 hooks in my experience, though these may appear smaller than the natural actually on the water at the time.

C. Egg-laying Sedge – Tying Sequence
1. Hook size 14 to 18.
2. Use a silk of a colour appropriate to the species being imitated. Wind the silk along the shank and about halfway round the bend.

Figure 28   Footprint Flies. Trichoptera. Egg-laying sedge.

3. Tie in a thin strand of green poly yarn or yellow Krystal Flash at the point halfway round the bend and form a small ball of eggs at this position. Tie off and trim (fig. 28).

4. Tie in poly yarn or Benecchi dub of the appropriate body colour against the egg ball. Wind the silk to the eye.

5. For wings take a piece of appropriately coloured poly yarn twice the length of the hook. Double the yarn into a V and tie in the apex of the V starting a short distance behind the eye. Continue tying in the wings and form a short thorax, but do not make it too long. The resulting wings should lie close along the top of the hook shaft. A stripped hackle post as used in the floating sedge is not required as the wings are used instead, as in the dun pattern.

6. Place a drop of Floo Gloo between the two wings at their base and place them in a gallows tool as for the dun so that they are vertical.

7. Tie in one or two pair of Betts' tailing fibres each side of the eye to act as antennae and balancers as in the floating sedge. Ensure they are well spread and pointing upwards.

8. Wind on the dub to the eye, tie off and trim. Make sure the dub is not too tight against the rear of the wing base as this will prevent the wings lying flat.

9. Tie in a hackle and allow the silk to hang down.

10. Use the wings as a post round which to wind the hackle but *reverse* the usual procedure for tying in the hackle, i.e. two turns to the front and only one to the back. Tie off using a hitch tool as described for the dun, being careful not to trap the antennae.

11. Cut off the hackles above the horizontal to the rear but leave the others at the sides and front.

12. Release the wings from the gallows tool and lay them parallel to the body. Place a drop of Floo Gloo at the base of the wings to lock in the hackle and keep the wings flattened. Stroke the wings with Floo Gloo to stiffen them a little and make sure they are separated by an angle of about 45°. Trim wings to an appropriate length with a V-form at the rear as for the floating sedge.

The position of the hackle forward of halfway along the hook shaft should result in the barb and egg ball being pushed below the water surface. To facilitate this, some artificial mud may be put on the egg ball and floatant on the hackle.

Diptera

General Dipteran Pattern – Tying Sequence
1.   Hook sizes 16 or 18.
2.   Tie in the appropriate colour of silk (black or green) and wind it slightly beyond the hook bend.
3.   To form the body tie in a strand of appropriately coloured poly yarn or Benecchi dub along with a length of Krystal Flash, yellow for black dubbing and red or pearl for green dubbing (fig. 29 A).
4.   Take the silk back to the eye.
5.   Take a length of white or buff poly yarn (about 2 cm is enough for a size 16 hook). Place the end of the yarn close to the eye and lay it along the top of the body. Tie it in starting at the eye and ending just forward of the middle of the hook. Place a drop of Floo Gloo on the tying.

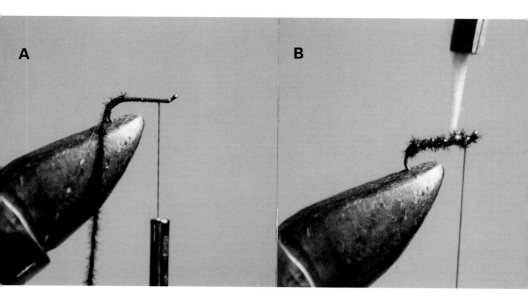

Figure 29   Footprint Fly. Diptera.

A. Hook with black poly yarn and yellow Krystal Flash tied in at the tail.

B. The wings are held in a gallows tool and the poly yarn and Krystal Flash ribbed body is completed.

Figure 29 cont.   C. Wings held in gallows tool and the hackle ready for winding.
D. Hackle fully wound and tied off.
E. Poly yarn wings held in vice to dry in position.
F. Fly on a water surface.
G. Fly seen through the window with the 'legs', wings and body colour all clearly visible.

6. Place the wings in a gallows tool.

7. Wind the black or green poly yarn or Benecchi dub to the eye, followed by the Krystal Flash, tie off and trim (fig. 29 B). Do not put too much yarn or dub behind the wings or it will later prove difficult to make them lie backwards at a low angle.

8. Tie in a hackle behind the eye and parallel with the hook (fig. 29 C). The hackle fibres should be slightly longer than normally used for the dun patterns: this gives stability to the fly as the longer hackle fibres above the horizontal act like tails or antennae.

9. Let the bobbin hang.

10. Wind the hackle as for the dun pattern and tie off using a hitch tool. Trim off excess hackle and silk. Place a drop of Floo Gloo at the base of the wings to lock in the hackle (fig. 29 D).

11. *Do not trim off any above-the-horizontal hackle fibres* since these fibres act as stabilisers as mentioned above.

12. Release the poly yarn from the gallows tool and separate it into two equal parts. Smear them with Floo Gloo to form horizontal broad wings by combing with a needle if necessary. When the wings are dry place a spot of Uhu glue under them and hold the wings down at a low angle to the hook shaft until the glue sets using the same method as for the floating sedge (fig. 29 D).

13. Trim the wings to a length which ends just beyond the hook bend. The wings should form a V pointing backwards at a low angle to the body and form an angle of about 45° to each other as for the floating sedge (fig. 29 E).

Testing the fly

Test the fly as for the dun and sedge. With the majority of the hackles still on, the fly should fall with the wings uppermost and land RWU but may not do so as consistently as the dun pattern. The fly should ride high on the water with the barb in the air (fig. 29 F). Yellow Krystal Flash over a black body gives a 'blue-bottle' green colour to the fly when seen from below which I believe fish find attractive, while pearl or red Krystal Flash used over green also offers a lot of contrast. A plain, slim black body should suffice for chironomid and midge patterns. Variations of this pattern, namely Black and Green 'Gnat', Hawthorn Fly and Midge will be found in Chapter 7.

Chapter 7

Patterns for Various Species

Ephemeroptera

(See Chapter 5 for specific details of the tying of ephemerid species.)

A. Mayfly – Black/Yellow Pattern (fig. 30)
1.   **Hook**. Size 12 to 16.
2.   **Tying silk**. Yellow.
3.   **Tails**. Two pairs of Betts' tailing fibres, each pair consisting of two fibres or more as appropriate.
4.   **Body**. Black and yellow poly yarn or black poly yarn and yellow Benecchi dubbing on a string (New Dub). The tip of the body is black and the rest, including the thorax, is yellow.
5.   **Wings**. Poly yarn buff (beige) or blue dun (grey dun or grey).
6.   **Hackle**. Grizzle or white. Usually the above-the-horizontal fibres are removed, but if white and left in place they should be stained with Studio Colour pens to match wings.

Figure 30 Footprint Flies. Ephemeroptera. Yellow/black Mayfly. White hackles have been used for photographic purposes but grizzle hackles are preferred.

7. **Head**. Form with silk.
8. **Finish**. Round the tips of the wings. Treat with Permafloat, Airflow Repel and Restore, Orvis Dry Floatant or similar. If using a dry powder floatant, such as Orvis Dry Floatant, do not treat the hackles with silicone grease, as the powder will stick to this when drying the fly after a take. I use silicone liquid for initial treatment and amadou plus drying powder for restoration after a catch.

B. Mayfly – Grey Body (fig. 31)
1. **Hook**. 14 to 16.
2. **Tying silk**. Grey.
3. **Tails**. Two pairs of Betts' tailing fibres, each pair consisting of two fibres or more as appropriate.
4. **Body**. Grey poly yarn or grey Benecchi dubbing brush.
5. **Wings**. Poly yarn buff (beige) or blue dun (grey dun or grey).
6. **Hackle**. Grizzle or white. Usually the above-the-

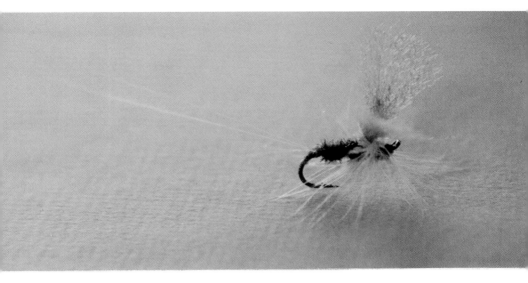

Figure 31 Grey Mayfly.

horizontal fibres are removed, but if white and left in place they should be stained with Studio Colour pens to match the wings.

7. **Head**. Form with silk.
8. **Finish**. As for pattern A.

C. Mayfly – Egg-laying female (see fig. 24)
1. **Hook**. 12 to 16.
2. **Tying silk**. As for pattern A.
3. **Tails**. As for pattern A.
4. **Body**. As for pattern A with the addition of an egg ball of green poly yarn or yellow Krystal Flash tied as described for Egg-laying Dun (see Chapter 5).
5. **Wings**. As for pattern A but set slightly further forwards (See Chapter 5).
6. **Hackle**. As for pattern A but the number of turns forwards and backwards are reversed compared to the normal (See Chapter 5).

7. **Head**. As for pattern A.
8. **Finish**. As for pattern A.

D. Mayfly – Spinner, Yellow or Grey Body (see fig. 25)
1. **Hook**. Size 12 to 16.
2. **Tying silk**. Yellow or grey.
3. **Tails**. Three Betts' tailing fibres (one central and two lateral horizontally in line with the hook shank).
4. **Body**. Yellow or grey poly yarn or Benecchi dub. The posterior tip of the body should be black or brown if the body is yellow.
5. **Wings**. Buff or grey poly yarn, tied spent.
6. **Hackle**. None, or a couple of turns, figure-of-eight fashion, using a grizzle hackle with top and bottom facing fibres removed. Too many fibres show up very starkly when the fly is viewed from below and are probably inhibiting to fish whereas their absence does not seem to have any effect.
7. **Head**. Form with silk.
8. **Finish**. Thin coat of Floo Gloo on wings to stiffen them. Round the tips of the wings. Comb wing tips if thick.

Figure 32   Mayfly emerger.

E. Mayfly – Emerging Adult (see fig. 32)

1.   **Hook**. Size 12 to 16.
2.   **Tying silk**. Yellow.
3.   **Tails**. Three Betts' tailing fibres (one central and two lateral horizontally in line with hook shank).
4.   **Body**. Buff, yellow or grey poly yarn or Benecchi dub.
5.   **Wings**. None.
6.   **Hackle**. None.
7.   **Head**. Form with silk.
8.   **Finish**. Shuck of mixed orange and red poly yarn or a bunch of pearl Krystal Flash fibres tied either, a. just behind the eye so as to lie over the body, or b. as a 'tail' tied in at the rear and wings added as in fig. 36. The former style should be stiffened slightly with Floo Gloo especially near the eye to keep the yarn in position.

Other Ephemeropteran Species

For these patterns refer to *Trout Fly Recognition* by J. Goddard for guidelines on colours to use for different species.

Figure 33   General Dun pattern. Only one pair of tails are shown but two pairs are preferable.

A. Dun (fig. 33)

1. **Hook**. Size 14 to 18 (size 16 preferred).
2. **Tying silk**. Colour to match species being imitated.
3. **Tails**. Four (or more) Betts' tailing fibres in two pairs widely spaced.
4. **Body**. Colour to match species being imitated.
5. **Wings**. Buff or grey poly yarn according to species being imitated.
6. **Hackle**. Grizzle or white. Usually the above-the-horizontal fibres are removed, but if white and left in place they should be stained with Studio Colours to match the wing colour.
7. **Head**. Form with silk.
8. **Finish**. Round the tips of the wings.

B. Spinner (fig. 34)

1. **Hook**. Size 14 to 18 (size 16 preferred).
2. **Tying silk**. Colour to match species being imitated.
3. **Tails**. Two or three Betts' tailing fibres widely spaced.

Figure 34 Footprint Flies. Ephemeroptera. Spinners. Bicolour variety on left and monocolour on right.

4. **Body**. Red, yellow, olive, insect green or black poly yarn. Two types of bodies are needed, namely the monocolour type with thorax and abdomen the same colour and the bicolour type with the thorax dark and the abdomen a lighter colour (yellow, red, olive or green). The two types are necessary as the Apricot, Pale Watery, and Little and Large Amber, Small and Large Spurwing, and Pale Evening Spinner fit into the monocolour type, while LDO, MO, Iron Blue, Claret Spinner, BWO, Sherry Spinner and Yellow Upright all belong to the bicolour type. Krystal Flash may be added if desired, yellow with black/red bodies, red with yellow/olive/insect green.
5. **Wings**. White or buff poly yarn.
6. **Hackle**. None or very sparse indeed.
7. **Head**. Form with silk.
8. **Finish**. Stiffen wings with light film of Floo Gloo and round off their ends.

C. Emerger Type 1 (fig. 35)
1. **Hook**. Size 14 to 18 (size 16 preferred).
2. **Tying silk**. Colour to match species being imitated.
3. **Tails**. None. Attach either two short bunches of unmixed red

Figure 35 Emerger Type 1.

and yellow poly yarn, or a bunch of yellow or pearl Krystal Flash to form a shuck.
4.   **Body**. Colour to match species being imitated. Yellow or pearl Krystal Flash may be used as ribbing if desired.
5.   **Wings**. None.
6.   **Hackle**. None, but if desired a grizzle or white hackle can be tied in a figure-of-eight fashion (about two turns). Trim off the central hackles above and below the hook shaft so that the body of the fly sits close to the water and the 'tail' (shuck) is in contact with or below the surface film.
7.   **Head**. Form with silk.
8.   **Finish**. None.

D. Emerger Type 2 (fig 36)

1.   **Hook**. Size 14 to 18 (size 16 preferred).
2.   **Tying silk**. Colour to match species being imitated.
3.   **Tails**. None. Attach a short bunch of separate red and yellow poly yarn or yellow or pearl Krystal Flash as a shuck.
4.   **Body**. Colour to match species being imitated.
5.   **Wings**. Buff or grey, depending on species, tied dun fashion but slightly nearer the eye as for Egg-laying Dun pattern, so that the shuck lies on the water surface.

Figure 36   Emerger Type 2.

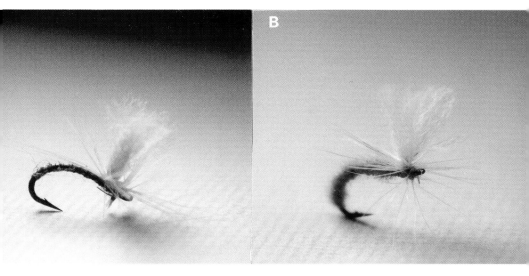

Figure 37   A. and B. Emerger type 3, Klinkhamer variation.

6.   **Hackle**. Grizzle or white. Usually the above-the-horizontal fibres are removed, but if white and left in place they should be stained with Studio Colour pens to match the wing colour.
7.   **Head**. Form with silk.
8.   **Finish**. Stiffen wings with a thin film of Floo Gloo. Round off the wing tips.

E. Emerger Type 3 (Modified Klinkhamer Special) (fig. 37 A and B)
1.   **Hook**. Sedge hook 14 to 18.
2.   **Tying silk**. To match species being imitated.
3.   **Tails**. None.
4.   **Body**. To match species being imitated. Green, yellow, red poly yarn or Benecchi dub and black poly yarn/dub with yellow Krystal Flash ribbing all seem to work well. Take the silk round the bend. Two body types are suggested:

  • Benecchi dub or poly yarn is started just below the top of the bend (so as not to reduce the hook gape), formed into a slightly thicker thorax and tied off behind the eye leaving a small space for finishing the head (fig. 37 B).

- Tie in a length of yellow Krystal Flash, form a body with the tying silk, make a thicker thorax, and then wind on the Krystal Flash, completely covering the silk underbody (fig. 37 A).

5. **Wings**. Two of appropriately coloured (not white) poly yarn just behind the eye as for the Egg-laying Mayfly dun pattern.
6. **Hackle**. Grizzle or white wound round the base of the wings *above* the hook shaft, i.e. no fibres beneath the hook shaft. Two turns is usually sufficient.
7. **Head**. Form with silk.
8. **Finish**. Trim wings and round tips. A drop of Floo Gloo is placed between and around the wings to seal in the hackle and keep the wings apart. The wings are stiffened with a film of Floo Gloo. The major length of the hook should sink below the water surface and give a double image in the mirror.

F. Egg-laying Dun
1. **Hook**. Size 14 to 18 (size 16 preferred).
2. **Tying Silk**. Colour to match species being imitated.
3. **Tails**. Two or three Betts' tailing fibres well spread and pointing upwards.
4. **Body**. Colour to match species being imitated. Use an egg ball of green poly yarn or yellow Krystal Flash tied in just round the bend of the hook.
5. **Wings**. These must be situated slightly forward of the normal position to ensure the rear of the hook dips below the water surface. The colour should be buff or grey poly yarn.
6. **Hackle**. Grizzle or white. Usually the above-the-horizontal fibres are removed, but if white and left in place they should be stained to match the wings using Studio Colour pens. The number of turns forwards and backwards is reversed (See Chapter 5.)
7. **Head**. Form with silk.
8. **Finish**. Stiffen the wings by wiping with Floo Gloo. Round off the wing tips.

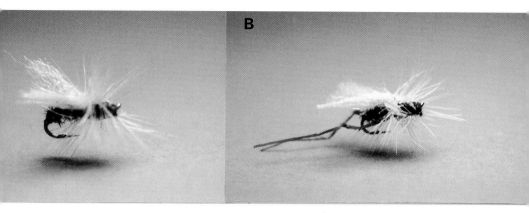

Figure 38   Footprint Flies. Diptera.
A. General dipteran pattern with black/yellow Krystal Flash body.
B. Hawthorn Fly.

Dipteran Species

A. Black or Green Gnat or Midge (fig. 38 A)
(See Chapter 6 for details of the tying of this pattern.)
1. **Hook**. Size 16 or 18.
2. **Tying silk**. Black or green.
3. **Tails**. None.
4. **Body**. Black poly yarn or Benecchi dub with yellow Krystal Flash for ribbing in both cases or green poly yarn and red Krystal Flash. For the midge pattern use black silk to give a slimmer body outline.
5. **Wings**. Buff poly yarn. The wings must be tied in tilted sharply backwards, and flattened horizontally.
6. **Hackle**. Grizzle wound round a hackle post. Leave on the above-the-horizontal fibres.
7. **Head**. Form with silk.
8. **Finish**. Round wing tips and stiffen with Floo Gloo.

Hawthorn Fly (fig. 38 B)
1. **Hook**. Size 16 to 18.
2. **Tying silk**. Black.

3. **Tails**. None.
4. **Body**. Black Benecchi dub or poly yarn with yellow Krystal Flash ribbing in both cases.
5. **Wings**. Buff poly yarn tied in as for dun.
6. **Hackle**. Grizzle wound round wings in Footprint Fly fashion. *Before* carrying out this operation fix two legs of knotted pheasant tail fibres training backwards underneath, or use knotted black poly yarn rolled into a thin tube and glued using Floo Gloo. Place the legs in hackle pliers and let them hang down, so as to keep the legs out of the way while winding the hackle.
7. **Head**. Form with silk.
8. **Finish**. Trim and round the wing tips and smear with Floo Gloo. Place a drop of Floo Gloo between the wings to fix the hackle and keep the wings apart.

Trichoptera

(See Chapter 6 for specific details of tying trichopteran patterns)

A. Adult Floating Sedge (fig. 39 A)

1. **Hook**. Size 12 to 16.
2. **Tying silk**. To match the body colour of the species being imitated, usually orange, grey, black, tan and green for the Grannom.
3. **Tails**. None.
4. **Body**. Either Benecchi dub or poly yarn to match the tying silk. Before winding the body on the shaft tie in a hackle post on which the hackle can be wound Footprint Fly fashion.
5. **Wings**. Poly yarn to match the colour of the tying silk. The wings must lie flat over the body and extend beyond the hook bend.
6. **Hackle**. Grizzle or white. Usually the above-the-horizontal fibres are left on except behind the wings and if white should be stained with Studio Colour pens to match the silk. Wind the hackle round the taut stripped hackle post.
7. **Head**. Add four Betts' tailing fibres in two pairs widely spaced each side of the hook eye as antennae.
8. **Finish**. Trim wings to a V-shape posteriorly and stiffen with a very thin film of Floo Gloo applied to the outer sides. Separate the wings at the rear.

Figure 39 Tricoptera. A. Grey Sedge. B. Spent Sedge. Only one pair of antennae is shown but two pairs are preferred.

C. Spent Sedge (fig. 39 B)

1. **Hook**. Size 14 to 16.
2. **Tying silk**. To match the species being imitated – orange, grey, black, tan or green.
3. **Tails**. None.
4. **Body**. Benecchi dub or poly yarn to match the tying silk (orange, grey, black, tan or green). Two pair of antennae using two Betts' tailing fibres can be added but their absence does not appear to reduce the attractiveness of this pattern.
5. **Wings**. Poly yarn of a colour to match the tying silk. Two pair of wings are formed, tied spent. Stiffen them with a film of Floo Gloo.
6. **Hackle**. None, or very sparse with upper and lower hackles removed so that the fly lies on or in the surface film.
7. **Head**. Form with silk.
8. **Finish**. Trim both wings so that the forward edge is longer than the posterior one, with the result that each pair is roughly triangular in shape with rounded corners.

D. Egg-laying Adult Sedge (fig. 40)

1. **Hook**. Size 12 to 16 sedge hook.
2. **Tying silk**. To match the body colour of the species being imitated, usually orange, grey, black, tan and green for the Grannom.
3. **Tails**. None.
4. **Body**. Place an egg ball halfway round the bend made of either green poly yarn or yellow Krystal Flash; the rest of the body should be either Benecchi dub or poly yarn to match the tying silk. No hackle post is needed.
5. **Wings**. Poly yarn to match the tying silk (orange, grey or black). These should be tied in slightly forward of the position normal for the floating sedge so that the egg ball and bend of the hook are below the water surface.
6. **Hackle**. Grizzle or white wound round the base of the wings. Leave on all the above-the-horizontal hackle fibres except for those under the wings and stain with appropriate Studio Colour pens if the hackle is white.
7. **Head**. Add four Betts' tailing fibres in two pairs, widely spaced each side of the eye as antennae.
8. **Finish**. Trim wings to a V-shape posteriorly and stiffen with

Figure 40   Egg-laying sedge.

a very thin film of Floo Gloo applied to the outer sides. Separate the wings at the rear.

E. Emerging Sedge (fig. 41)
1. **Hook**. Size 12 to 16.
2. **Tying silk**. To match the colour of the species being imitated (orange, grey, black, tan or green).
3. **Tails**. Short length of yellow and red poly yarn (unmixed) or yellow or pearl Krystal Flash. This represents the shuck and the slightly forward position of the wings should ensure it always touches the water surface.
4. **Body**. Benecchi dub or poly yarn of a colour to match the tying silk. No hackle post is needed.
5. **Wings**. Poly yarn of a colour to match the tying silk. Tie in as for egg-laying sedge pattern.

Figure 41   Emerger sedge. Only one pair of antennae is shown but two pairs are to be preferred.

6.   **Hackle**. Grizzle or white wound round wings as for egg-laying sedge pattern.

7.   **Head**. Form with silk. Add two pair of Betts' tailing fibres as antennae.

8.   **Finish**. Trim the wings to a V at the rear and ensure they slope backwards. Stiffen with a smear of Floo Gloo and make sure they are separated at the rear.

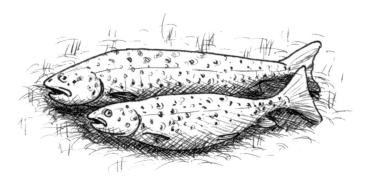

Chapter 8

Back to the Beginning

In this book the emphasis in the development of new fly patterns has been transferred from the prey to the hunter. Previously the main criteria which influenced fly patterns were the characteristics of the prey insect in the various stages of its life cycle. Consequently, though patterns ranged from the suggestive to the exact, it was the morphology of the adult or larval insect as it impinged upon the eye of *Homo sapiens*, rather than that of *Salmo trutta* which determined the appearance of any particular pattern. In contrast, the tyings described in this text have been determined by a simple principle, namely that the manner in which the trout sees and responds to the natural fly must be the deciding factors in the creation of an artificial. As Marinaro wrote when discussing the difficulty of defining a 'strict imitation' in *A Modern Dry-Fly Code*, 'above all it cannot be done in the way of Halford, Ronalds and others of ancient fame, for they spoke in terms of human vision and comprehension, supported only by the prop of entomology. That way alone lies great error, since it does not take into account the visions of the trout and the geometry of the underwater world.'

101

What the fisherman observes of the floating fly from above the water surface is of almost no significance; what matters are the images which the trout perceives in mirror and window. To the fisherman the fly attached to his leader may appear aesthetically satisfying, be a good imitation of nature's model and prove itself an excellent floater but these characteristics are as nought if that fly does not give the correct signals in the correct order to the feeding trout. Consequently, the primary consideration when devising any new pattern must be 'How will the trout see it and will it stimulate its predatory instincts?'

Before we tie an artificial, therefore, we must put ourselves mentally into the trout's brain and look about its environment through its eyes. Hence the emphasis in the early chapters of this book on the anatomical, physiological and visual properties of the piscean eye and that eye's inherent advantages and limitations for an aquatic dweller like the trout. The retailing of such information, which at first sight may appear to be irrelevant to tying an artificial fly, is in fact paramount. Without the knowledge of the properties and functions of the fish's eye and the interaction of light rays with that ubiquitous fluid, water, we would have no sound foundation for devising an effective artificial from first principles. Without the scientific facts, we would not know which are and which are not the significant features which an artificial fly should present to our quarry or to which our quarry would instinctively react in the way we desire, that is by taking our hook into its mouth.

In attempting to create a more effective fly without such specific information, we would replace an informed choice by guess-work, trial and error and experience, all time-consuming activities unable to guarantee a solution to our problem. It is true, of course, that successful dry flies have evolved or been developed without reference to scientific knowledge of trout vision or the physical properties of light. Careful study and casual observation of the natural history of aquatic and terrestrial insects and the activities of trout in relation to them by both river-keepers and fishermen have led to the production of patterns which have passed the test of time. In the classical collection, flies such as Lunn's Particular, Lunn's Yellow Boy, Invicta, GHRE, Wickham's Fancy, Tups, Red Tag and Pheasant Tail spring readily to mind. Some of these flies are winged, some are not, some are close imitations of a particular insect while others are only suggestive of many. However, the evolution of these patterns has been long and somewhat haphazard and perhaps the reasons for their success should now be subject to scrutiny in the spotlight of current knowledge, so as to highlight the particular characteristics of them which trout find appetizing. That perhaps is a project for another author. So though classical patterns may still justify their place in the fly box, perhaps they should be looked at from a new viewpoint. In any case the rationale for developing new patterns or modifying old ones should still lie within the sphere of the scientific approach advocated and practised in these pages.

It is an unhappy fact that the majority of fishermen do not have a lifetime to spend in observing the minutae of a trout's life and feeding habits or have the leisure to become expert entomologists and so in the past have had to rely on the accumulated experience of fisherman as a group over a long period. Unfortunately, as we all know, such acquired wisdom of the ages can sometimes be tainted with personalities, prejudices and particular circumstances which lend a certain unreliability to the so-called 'facts' which become the accepted wisdom. However, we are now at a point where soundly-based scientific knowledge can be brought to bear on the problem of developing more effective flies and that knowledge can be easily acquired. As fishermen we would be unwise to neglect such information or fail to give it the true status it deserves in our thinking relative to the origination of new fly patterns or the efficacy of old ones.

Clearly only a scientific and rational attitude to the development of new dry-fly patterns will ensure even a modicum of success at the water. Every fisherman knows that a certain pattern will tempt some foolish fish sometime, presumably because it has at least one of the characteristics of the natural which will attract a trout's attention. Even this supposition is subject to doubt, however, for trout sometimes take the oddest 'food' into their stomach, including it appears even the cork tip of a cigarette! Nevertheless if the fisherman is unaware as to why the victim fell last time and why another fish might do so again, then fishing becomes a chuck-and-chance-it operation, not hunting in the true sense of the word. Many of the real satisfactions of fishing are negated by the marked uncertainty underlying such an approach to angling with an artificial fly. Any fly-fisher is denying himself innumerable opportunities for pleasure by neglecting to inform himself of the pertinent factors the trout uses to determine if a fly, real or imitation, is worthy of its attention.

Happily for the fishing fraternity, there is an unknown variable in the fishing equation. Even if a purely scientific approach allowed the production of a perfect imitation giving all the right signals in the right sequence (an improbable proposition in itself), it would not ensure the pattern would invariably be taken. The final decision forever lies with the trout and its instincts. So even though all the necessary stimuli are presented to the fish, it may at that moment be of perverse mind, or want another fly species, or have a full stomach, or perhaps not be in hunting mode or have any other valid fishy reason to the fore which is beyond our ken! I, personally, would not have it any other way, for a fish hooked each and every cast would be hell, not heaven, as the familiar fisherman's joke relates.

However an understanding of a fish's vision of the underwater and above water worlds and the uncertainties of a trout's mental processes, are not the only factors which must be considered when developing a new pattern; there are two others, the pattern itself and the fisherman who ties it. Each of the materials used in a pattern has physical properties and characteristics of its own and when certain of them are combined together the result may have other attributes, since the whole may be greater than the sum of its parts! Each material utilised may have intrinsic advantages or limitations and determine the methods used to produce a certain end result. An excellent example of this has been my own attempt to use Lacewing, a plastic winging material, in some of the patterns given in this book. Though the wings looked very realistic and the flies seemed to perform well when dropped at home, I was unable to prevent duns and spinners revolving frantically when cast and turning a tippet into a nightmare tangle after only a cast or two; perhaps others will succeed, I hope so. However, the choice of materials and the method of tying are largely predetermined by the factors to which allusion has already been made, namely the sequence of visual events which stimulate the trout to rise and take. For example when devising a system for winding on a hackle the primary question will be whether the system chosen gives the correct 'footprint' on the water. Of course there are secondary considerations, such as whether the hackle will prove stiff enough to support the fly on the water so that the barb is in the air, or that the hackle fibres should not be so stiff that they penetrate the surface film instead of resting on it, or that the colour of the hackle is appropriate. Similarly with artificial wings the important quality of the material used and the method of tying must be determined by the requirement of 'wing flash' and a certain transparency so that the spectrum of Snell's circle can 'colour' the wings at the appropriate time. Consequently in the final analysis, even the choice of materials and tying technique is controlled by the trout's vision of its world. An additional factor is the durability of materials in use and of the fly itself, for a fly which comes to pieces after a few casts or the first take is a frustration and a great waste of time spent at the vice. This can be a limiting factor in the choice of materials and the evolution of new patterns, as I have found along with many another fishermen.

What of the other factor, the fly tier himself. He can certainly prove a severe limitation if he lacks knowledge of basic fly tying methods or is without the necessary dexterity. In my view the inventor of any new pattern should keep in mind the average fisherman who is not an expert in the art of creating artificial flies and may not even be an experienced tier of flies. I confess that I readily accepted this admonition, for I personally am not particularly dextrous and average would certainly describe my fly tying ability most aptly. Consequently I have tried in the patterns described in this book to keep them as simple as possible, though I accept the sedge and dipteran patterns do present certain difficulties with respect to wings and hackling. However, I do not think even these patterns are beyond the skill of the average fly tier and should allow him to produce consistently artificials of the required quality and quantity. Hopefully some readers will have the inspiration to improve on the methods of tying these sedge, dipteran, and, perhaps, other patterns too.

Despite their advantages, the patterns described in this book, especially the ephemeridian and trichopterous imitations, do have one overriding drawback. The extensive tails of the former and the long antennae of the latter make the flies bulky, so that only a large fly box with ample compartments can accommodate them. This means that only two or three flies can be lodged together in one compartment and the larger fly boxes which are needed cannot easily be kept in a fishing jacket pocket. However such a handicap is unavoidable if the essential characteristics of the flies which the trout requires are to be attained. Unhappily for fly-fishermen no compromise is available, for our target being a hunter itself is quite adamant in its demands! Nevertheless, I believe that the simpler and easier the techniques required to tie a pattern with gives the correct signals in the correct sequence the better for all concerned, tier, fisherman and fish! Consequently it is my hope that this text will prove a stimulus to more inventive minds than my own and that these patterns will turn out to be mere stepping stones to other improved, but easier to tie, patterns in the future. It surely cannot be otherwise!

Bibliography

Clark, B. and Goddard, J. (1980) *The Trout and the Fly*. Earnest Benn

Goddard, J. (1966) *Trout Fly Recognition*. A & C Black

Marinaro, V.C. (1970) *A Modern Dry Fly Code*. Crown

Marinaro, V.C. (1976) *In the Ring of the Rise*. Crown

Pumphrey, R.J. (1961) *Concerning Vision in The Cell and the Organism*. Ramsey, J.A. and Wigglesworth, V.B. (Eds) Cambridge Univ. Press

Roberts, J. (1988) *To Rise a Trout*. The Crowood Press

Wakeford, J. (1980) *Flytying Techniques*. A & C Black

Wakeford, J. (1991) *Flytying Tools and Materials*. A & C Black

Walls, G.L. (1942) *The Vertebrate Eye*. Boomfield Hills, Michigan. Crown Brook Institute

Ward, F. (1919) *Animal Life Underwater*. Cassell

Witlock, D. (1982) *Guide to Aquatic Trout Foods*. Benn

Index

Index